"Having traveled with Dr. Williams on several international disaster trips, I can attest to the need for preparation, flexibility, and sensitivity to the leading of the Holy Spirit in these situations! These are tremendous opportunities to share the Gospel, and Dr. Williams's experience and expertise make him the right one to help us all be more prepared for future disaster response efforts."

-Mitch W. Duininck, M.D.
Residency Director, In His Image

"Dr. Paul Williams has poured out the Love of Jesus through his medical missionary work in over 105 countries, sacrificing his life in a living testimony to answer the high calling that is in Christ Jesus. Tens of thousands have come to the Lord through his ministry. I have never met a finer man, the embodiment of a true Christian."

-Gabe Rizzi, M.D.,
General and Vascular Surgery

"I have known and worked with Dr. Paul Williams for over 18 years in medical missions. He has a deep compassion for the poor and hurting peoples of the world and a heart for them to receive care for the whole person, meeting their medical, physical, and spiritual needs. He has been a pioneer in the development of global medical missions, including disaster relief missions. Providing relief in disasters such as the typhoon in Bangladesh, the tsunami in Banda Aceh, Indonesia, earthquakes and hurricanes in Central America, and the refugee camps of Rwanda has given him a wealth of experience from which he can share with us (the reader) about disaster preparedness."

-Chris Feucht, M.D.
Director of Missions, New Life Ministries Int'l

D0180336

What others have said about Dr. Paul Williams and *When All Plans Fail*:

"Dr. Paul Williams is uniquely qualified to write a book on disaster preparedness. He has organized and led medical teams, including teams from our own In His Image International, in a number of major world disasters since the early 1990s. From the refugee camps created by the Rwandan Civil War to hurricane-ravaged Central America to tsunami devastation and earthquakes around the world, he has been there.

Leading teams into these areas of desperate need and destruction makes him practically experienced so that his recommendations on preparedness ring out as someone who has 'been there, done that.' And Dr. Williams in print is like Dr. Williams as a real-life team leader, a man who cares to give God's very best."

-John R. Crouch Jr., M.D.
President, In His Image International

"The Bible speaks of the shaking of our day. Paul Williams has dedicated his life to helping those in need during their time of shaking. There are very few men alive in the Body of Christ today who have the authority to speak about this shaking from the practical perspective given in Paul's book, *When All Plans Fail.* This book is written with revelation gleaned from a life of dedication to Christ, study of God's Word, and the experience of ministering to the poor in over 100 nations. I recommend Paul Williams, his life before God, and this book. It is a book for our time."

--Paul Cuny
President, Marketplace Leadership International

"I have known Paul Williams for over 40 years. He is a man with a heart for missions and people. It has been impressive to observe his vision as a medical missionary. His experience in over 100 nations with disaster relief work makes him well qualified to speak on the very important and relevant subject of disaster preparedness."

--Admiral Vernon E. Clark
USN (Ret.), Chief of Naval Operations (CNO)

"Many of us have gone through our entire lives without having to deal with a major disaster. Paul has purposely put himself in the middle of more than one disaster in order to bring living hope to those in need. Paul brings the healing gifts of a physician, the administrative gift of a leader, and a Christ-like love for those who are suffering. He freely brings these gifts right into the middle of some of the greatest disasters this world has known. His experience in responding to the tsunami of 2004 in Sumatra, Indonesia, alone more than qualifies him to bring us this insightful look into our role and responsibility. Whether man-made or natural, the word *disaster* seems more and more a part of our life. Now Paul is challenging us to step forward and be prepared."

-Mickey Salvant
CEO Shippers Service Company

"Dr. Paul Williams and I first met when he headed up the pioneer team (I was part of this team) that volunteered to help with the refugee crisis in Goma, Zaire, during the Rwandan war between the Hutus and Tutsis in the summer of 1994. We have subsequently been on teams to East and West Africa. His life and ministry demonstrated the principles of Jesus Christ on each of these trips.

His exemplary leadership, coupled with his humility, compassion and knowledge of international and cross-cultural effective disaster management is a great asset to our generation."

-Dora Akuetteh-Saforo, M.D., FAAFP

"Dr. Paul Williams is one of the finest medical missionaries today. We have worked side by side many times in Latin America and in Africa where the needs are overwhelming. He is a tireless and compassionate servant who knows how to minister the love of God through medicine and I am proud to call him a brother and friend!"

-Paul Wilbur
Artist, Integrity Music

WHEN ALL PLANS FAIL

BE READY FOR DISASTERS

by

PAUL R. WILLIAMS, M.D.

Published by Mountain View Publishing, L.L.C.
Pisgah Forest, NC, U.S.A.
www.whenallplansfail.com

Second Edition

Printed in the United States of America

ISBN: 978-0-615-20937-1

2 3 4 5 6 7 8 9 10 / 16 15 14 13 12 11 10

To Sofia
My Ukrainian Rose

CONTENTS

ACKNOWLEDGMENTS

When asked how long it took to write *When All Plans Fail*, my first response was, "Less than two months." As I reflect on that statement now, I realize that the true answer should have been, "My entire life." I am indebted to literally thousands of individuals who have impacted my life, through teaching, wise counsel, training, and by example. My heritage and immediate family gave me a solid foundation, but my writing has also been influenced by the people I have had the privilege of meeting in more than 105 nations around the world. The team members who joined me on more than two hundred mission trips are intricately woven into my heart.

Rising from the obscure background of a frightened little refugee girl who immigrated with her family to the United States to become my "Ukrainian Rose," my wife Sofia has been at my side throughout the many years of medical training, practice and my 25 years of medical mission ministry. She gave me our four wonderful children and managed the home front, making it possible for me to do the work to which I felt called. Sofia has willingly endured the lonely weeks when I sequestered myself for long periods to write. She became my primary prayer partner, convinced, even as I was, that the writing of the book needed to be directed by the Holy Spirit from beginning to end. Honey, thank you for being a constant source of encouragement through the best of times and the most challenging of times.

While in its embryonic form, Mary Bopp instantly "caught the vision" for the book upon hearing about it and gave her gracious and generous assistance so that I could begin. I am so deeply grateful to you, Mary, for your obedience to the inner prompting that you felt.

I owe special thanks to Don Wise for his "wise" counsel, providing incisive comments at very critical junctures in the publication process. Don was able to catch the vision I had for the book cover and translate it into an impactful message. I am deeply appreciative for his tireless personal efforts in behalf of this book. I also owe a debt of thanks to Ann Severance, who persevered in tirelessly editing the manuscript in record time. I am extremely grateful to her for taking this project on as a "special calling."

ACKNOWLEDGMENTS

There were other individuals who significantly contributed to this project from the onset because they believed in the message of the book and believed it was worthy of backing. Maryjo, my sister, who has been like a Miriam to me, has fully embraced the message of the role of the church and individual believers in disaster preparedness. Maryjo, my brother John, and I have become a team in this endeavor. I owe special thanks to my brother-in-law and sister-in-law, Don and Nina Helms, for their constant faith in me and for the support they have given.

In the process of writing this book, I have greatly benefited from the counsel, encouragement and support of the incredibly talented people that make up the board of International HealthCare Network. A special thank you is in order to our home prayer group, without whose constant support and prayers as challenges arose, we would not be where we are. I want to extend a heartfelt thank you to Carl and Juanita Phillips for their graciousness in providing a "getaway" to write the book. I also am extremely grateful to those who read the manuscript and have furnished insightful suggestions and provided much needed encouragement.

No one has enriched my life more than our three sons, Jim, Joseph and David, our daughter Debbie, their spouses, and our grandchildren. You bring deep meaning to life itself. You make me a very wealthy man!

Lastly, I gratefully acknowledge my Lord, who has stirred me deeply to share with you about the preparation we must make as believers to stand strong in the face of future storms so that we are ready to help our families and others.

INTRODUCTION

When All Plans Fail was written to challenge you to be prepared to face emergencies and disasters, both natural and man-made. The Hurricane Katrina disaster of 2005 revealed major weaknesses in local, regional and national disaster response planning. Some of the planned responses failed because the magnitude of the disaster outstripped the ability of first responders to reach many of those in need of help.

In this book I have emphasized the need for individuals and neighborhoods to take responsibility for their own preparedness and not to rely on governmentally established emergency programs alone.

In a 2004 survey conducted by the American Red Cross and Wirthlin Worldwide, only about 20 percent of Americans feel "very prepared" for a catastrophic event. That same survey found that only 10 percent of American households have developed a family emergency plan, have organized a disaster emergency kit, or have received training in first aid and CPR.

American Red Cross President and CEO Marsha Evans has commented, "We need to narrow the universe of the unprepared—those we need to worry about in catastrophic situations. Every one of those unprepared Americans is a potential barrier to the effectiveness of our response to disaster."

BE PREPARED, DON'T BE A VICTIM

If you have not prepared for emergencies and disasters, you have an increased likelihood of becoming a victim who will need assistance. First-responders to disasters focus on people who are injured, trapped or unable to help themselves. The larger the universe of prepared individuals and families, the more effective the disaster response will be. In fact, those who are prepared will often be in a position to help others and not be a drain on rescue efforts.

While researching the material for this book, I found an almost overwhelming amount of information written on the subject of disaster preparedness. And I'm a physician with experience in disaster relief! As a result, I felt the need to pull together a practical reference guide to preparing for times of crisis.

In my search of the literature, I was particularly struck by a comment made by Lt. General Russel Honoré, former commander of the Joint

Task Force-Katrina, at an American Military University symposium in February of 2007. General Honoré indicated that part of the preparedness issue lies in incomplete emergency planning. "Did you take your understanding of the disaster to failure?"

His question raised another in my mind: "What does one do 'when all plans fail'?" That, in fact, is exactly what was experienced during the 9-11 and Katrina tragedies. Individual preparedness would have made the difference between life and death for a number of people who perished.

When planning for a potential disaster, think practically. Anticipate what natural disasters you are most likely to encounter. Be prepared to help your family and neighbors; it may be days before governmental and community first responders can assist you. Approach preparation from a standpoint of doing the prudent thing, not from a basis of fear.

GOOD PLANNING WILL HELP RELIEVE MUCH ANXIETY

For some time I have felt the need to address the issue of disaster preparedness from a Christian perspective. Why Christians? Doesn't everyone need to be ready for emergencies? The answer is, of course, yes. However, those who believe in the God of the Bible, have a personal faith in Jesus Christ, and accept that the Bible is true, have a unique worldview. In *When All Plans Fail* you will find examples of how to network more effectively with family, friends, and neighbors—showing the love of Jesus—even before disasters occur.

In Chapter 8, I give several examples of churches and ministries that are being used as "salt" and "light" in their communities and beyond. It is my hope that some of these examples will challenge you, your pastor, and your entire church community. Maybe you will become one of the "transformers" of Chapter 9 as you join in extending compassionate ministry and advocating disaster preparedness.

In times of crisis, Christians and the church can and should play a unique role in responding to those in need. The church is a natural haven of refuge in troubled times.

The purpose of *When All Plans Fail* is not to examine the theological aspects of the return of Jesus, which for many is a point of contentious debate. We can, however, all agree that it is prudent to be prepared for the natural disasters that may pose a threat in the regions where we live, as well as man-made disasters, including acts of terrorism, should they occur.

In researching this book, I came across the story of a man who worked in New York City's Twin Towers during the time of the first bombing of the World Trade Center. After that tragic incident, he planned an escape route for himself should a similar disaster occur again. When the plane struck his building on September 11, 2001, the man was trapped on one of the floors above the point of impact. Heeding the warning and following his pre-determined plan, he was one of the few in that section of the building to make it out alive.

Sadly, many in New Orleans did not heed the warnings or develop a plan for handling a break in the levees. The possibility of such a breach had been discussed years before the disaster actually happened. Yes, there were governmental snafus, but individual preparedness could have resulted in a lower death toll.

In Addendum One, I have addressed questions about how the Department of Homeland Security plans to respond to future disasters, particularly when they reach the magnitude of 9-11 or Katrina.

In Addendum Two, you will learn about the existing networks in your community. These agencies welcome volunteers who will contribute to both the ongoing social service needs of the community as well as participate in emergency and disaster planning.

In times of crisis, people often ask the question "Why?" or "Why me?", searching for a deeper meaning to what has just occurred. Since many look to God and the Bible at such times, Christians and the church need to be ready to guide them to the Answer!

God still speaks to people through His Word, through others and directly to individual hearts. At times, He warns of impending danger and offers comfort and solace to those who are distressed and hurting. Through prayer, people are often healed physically and spiritually. And God chooses to use you and me to accomplish these things in His name! His plans never fail!

Many are the plans in a man's heart,
but it is the Lord's purpose that prevails.
—Proverbs 19:21

It is my sincere desire that if you are not yet adequately prepared to face emergencies and disasters, *When All Plans Fail* will help prepare you to weather future storms.

—Paul R. Williams, M.D.
Pisgah Forest, North Carolina

PART ONE

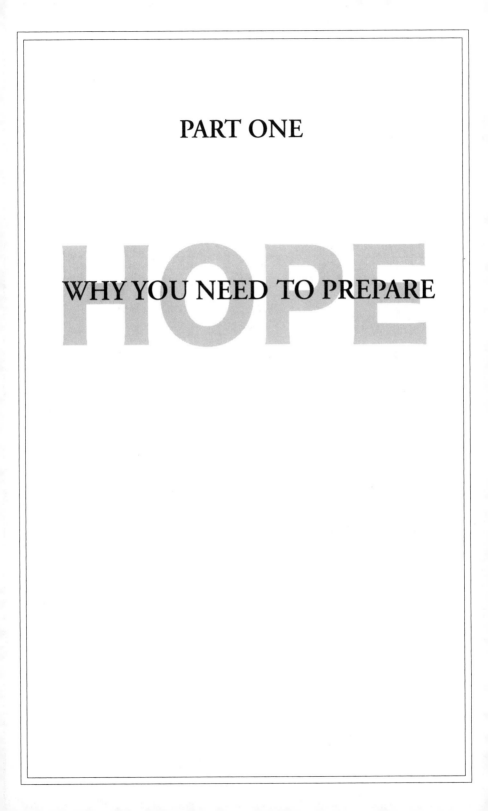

WHY YOU NEED TO PREPARE

THE SHEPHERD BOY AND THE WOLF

A young shepherd boy who cared for the village sheep entertained himself by crying, "Wolf!" when there was no wolf. Villagers would come to his rescue only to find out the alarms were false and they had wasted their time. After doing this a number of times, the villagers ignored the shepherd boy's cries.

One day a wolf did attack the sheep and the boy's cries for help went unheeded by the villagers and his sheep were killed.

The moral of the story:

Even when liars tell the truth, they are never believed. The liar will lie once, twice, and then perish when he tells the truth.

–Aesop's Fable

CHAPTER 1

IF YOU CRY "WOLF!" ONE MORE TIME
FACING FUTURE STORMS

In the story of the shepherd boy, I can just hear an irate villager threatening, "If you cry, 'Wolf!' one more time when there is no wolf in sight, I'll thrash you within an inch of your life!"

Many have grown weary of prophetic voices proclaiming that the end of the world is near. Some sects have even encouraged their members to sell all their worldly possessions and simply wait for the return of Jesus, only to have the "prophets" proven false. Such experiences have cast a long negative shadow on true prophetic voices and biblical truths, causing many to doubt the Scriptures.

It is not only prophetic voices that some people have turned a deaf ear to. The hysteria that swirled around Y2K for several years before January 1, 2000, left many people skeptical. Others claim major disasters were averted due to the incredible efforts made to minimize any negative impact. No matter what the actual facts were, no calamity occurred, and many families found themselves with unneeded generators, food, and emergency supplies that only made a dent in their wallets.

Many Christians were particularly susceptible to the letdown following Y2K. In their minds the year 2000 signaled the return of Christ, and when He didn't make an appearance and none of the other dire predictions came true, the whole scenario was reminiscent of someone crying, "Wolf!" I can also hear the echo of the old adage, "Fool me once, shame on you; fool me twice, shame on me!"

It is becoming increasingly difficult to pick up a newspaper or to turn on the TV without being bombarded by a steady barrage of bad news from around the world. Who wants to see dirty, malnourished children with bloated bellies? Who wants to hear about genocide in Rwanda, Liberia, and the Sudan, or sectarian fighting around the world? Daily newscasts feature explicit stories of people dying in the Middle East, Iraq, Afghanistan and other nations normally stable such as Kenya. And now we listen to the daily terrorism level in our own country, reported by the Department of Homeland Security. Fear and unease are on the rise in America.

Medically speaking, I can understand these feelings. A constant state of anticipation wears a person down emotionally. Media often plays to our fears since sensationalism promotes sales and viewership. This is not only true in the secular world, it is also true in the so-called Christian world. Many teachers and preachers tell people what they want to hear, not what they need to hear.

Yet burying our heads in the sand doesn't make problems go away, and avoidance prevents us from dealing with situations that could have a more favorable outcome if adequate preparations are made.

ON THE OTHER HAND…

I really enjoy the movie,"Fiddler on the Roof." Reptavia, the father, was quite a philosopher. In the play, he is fond of saying, "The Good Book says…but on the other hand!"

There are always two sides to every issue. Invariably, Jesus' advice was both practical and profound. On the one hand, He said, "Don't borrow from tomorrow's problems. You have your hands full with today's!" On the other hand, He gave us some pretty specific signs to look for at the time of His return. Both truths must be held in constant tension without one truth nullifying the other.

It is possible to hold these two truths simultaneously and function well. But some, I find, are almost paralyzed with fear and obsess over what might happen to affect their ability to live a normal life. Still others simply refuse to talk about prophecy, considering the topic either too controversial or irrelevant. Opinions vary widely, even among biblical scholars and teachers.

And then there is the matter of ordinary, everyday stress. Teenagers, young married couples with or without children, single parents, grandparents, widows—the list goes on. All of them face different challenges. What is a person to do? Is it possible to keep everything in balance?

Even without doomsday predictions, terrorism and tornadoes, flooding, fires, and drought—we need to plan carefully to meet everyday emergencies. The secret is to live one day at a time. LIVE in the NOW, but PREPARE for the FUTURE.

This is true spiritually as well as physically. We are told not to fear, no matter what appears on the horizon. This can only happen when the Prince of Peace, Jesus, gives us His peace. The peace He offers is not like anything the world knows. It is a peace that can keep one calm in the very midst of a storm! This peace is available to all true believers—those who place their trust in Him.

ARE YOU READY?

The truth of the matter is that the majority of people have not adequately planned for common everyday crises, whether or not they reach the level of disasters. Let me ask you some practical questions that, if not answered in the affirmative, will often result in frustration and loss of valuable time and resources…or worse:

- Do you keep jumper cables in the trunk of your car?

- Do you keep flashlights with good batteries on hand, or do you have flashlights that do not require batteries?

- Do you keep an umbrella in your car?

- Do you have surge protectors for your critical electrical appliances and office equipment?

- Do you carry your computer in a properly padded case or handbag?

- Do you cover your sensitive plants to protect them from the cold when a freeze warning is issued?

- Do you wear protective clothing if you are going to do outside work where you know you will encounter poison ivy?

- Do you take along extra water when jogging or riding your bicycle on long excursions?

- Do you avoid lifting objects too heavy for you?

- Do you change the oil in your car on the recommended schedule?

- Do you have health insurance (if you can afford it?)

- Do you have life insurance (if you can afford it?)

- Do you have homeowners insurance?

- Do you pray every day?

- Do you read the Bible every day?

Practical things. Everyday things. No hype, no fear. Just doing what is practical and prudent.

You probably answered yes to many of these, if not most. In this same spirit, you can prepare for potential disasters in a way that will make you prepared and ready rather than a victim—and help others who can't help themselves (see Chapter 7).

THE WOLF *WILL* COME!

When thinking of all the possible "wolves" you might have to face in your lifetime, what is the worst you can imagine? Most people do not list natural or physical storms as the worst disasters. Instead, they mention loss of loved ones or their own life or perhaps some kind of permanent disability or chronic illness.

But are there worse calamities? The Bible says there are.

And how does a man benefit if he gains the whole world and loses his soul in the process?

—Mark 8:36 (TLB)

Do not be afraid of those who kill the body but cannot kill the soul. Rather, be afraid of the One who can destroy both soul and body in hell.

—Matthew 10:28

Believers know—and want others to know—that there is something far worse than physical death. It is spiritual death. The death of the body is an enemy; make no mistake. But it is an enemy—"the last enemy," according to the Word of God—that will be destroyed. Those who believe in Jesus as their personal Savior will one day live forever with God in heaven. There will be no more tears. No more wars. No more death. This is Good News! This is the great hope that allows believers to face any storm.

When facing tragedies of any kind, God offers His protection. In 1994 I was part of the disaster relief response to the Rwandan refugees in

Goma, Zaire. Between 500,000 to one million Hutus and Tutsis had lost their lives in that genocidal conflict. Not knowing what to expect, I felt a quivering of apprehension in my belly.

On the flight to Goma, I was prompted to read over and over again Psalm 91:

> *He who dwells in the shelter of the Most High*
> *will rest in the shadow of the Almighty.*
> *I will say of the Lord, "He is my refuge*
> *and my fortress, my God, in whom I trust."*
> *Surely he will save you from the fowler's snare*
> *and from the deadly pestilence.*
> *He will cover you with his feathers,*
> *and under his wings you will find refuge;*
> *his faithfulness will be your shield and rampart.*
> *You will not fear the terror of night,*
> *nor the arrow that flies by day,*
> *nor the pestilence that stalks in the darkness,*
> *nor the plague that destroys at midday.*
> *A thousand may fall at your side,*
> *ten thousand at your right hand,*
> *but it will not come near you.*

—Psalm 91:1-7

The day I arrived with my medical team from Operation Blessing, 10,000 bodies lined the dusty roads leading out of Goma. The truth of the Scriptures leaped out at me. I had always thought of verse 7 figuratively, but that day it was a reality! For over two hours we drove at a snail's pace, dead bodies piled on either side of the road. There are no words to describe what we saw that day. Looking out over that horrific sight, I wept, my heart aching. I wondered how we could possibly make a difference.

The team I was leading worked under the United Nations High Commissioner for Refugees (UNHCR) and was assigned to Doctors Without Borders from Belgium. After working together for several days, one of their relief workers commented: "When I came here, I said to myself, 'God is not in this place!' But after seeing your team, I know that God is here!"

We could speak neither French nor the local Ngala language. We could only work feverishly, quietly praying, with death and disease all around us. In the next six months, sixty thousand people died of cholera, dysentery and other diseases in those camps, yet not one of our team became ill!

After several weeks, the refugees erected a church tent, naming the church, "God Walks In This Place." Only God could give such hope.

No doubt many have asked, "Where was God during 9-11 or when the levees broke after Katrina hit?" May I remind you that He often works best through His people? The single largest group of volunteers to respond to the disasters was officially reported as "faith-based." Many of you were there, serving as the hands and arms of Jesus. You were making the Invisible God visible.

The thought of disaster preparedness is daunting. Where will I find the time? Where do I go to get the proper information? How does the system of disaster response work in my local area and how is it coordinated with state and national programs? Will my preparation for disasters make a real difference? Why prepare?

THE SENSIBLE MAN

"A sensible man watches for problems ahead and prepares to meet them. The simpleton never looks, and suffers the consequences."

—Proverbs 27:12 (TLB)

For Want of a Nail

For want of a nail, the shoe was lost.
For want of a shoe, the horse was lost.
For want of a horse, the rider was lost.
For want of a rider, the battle was lost.
For want of a battle, the kingdom was lost.
And all for the want of a horseshoe nail.

—Benjamin Franklin

Maxims to Remember:

"To fail to plan is to plan to fail."

"An ounce of prevention is worth a pound of cure."

—Benjamin Franklin

CHAPTER 2

FOR WANT OF A NAIL
WHY PREPARE?

The wisdom of being prepared for foreseeable difficulties, natural, and even man-made disasters is pretty obvious. The proverb "For Want of a Nail" illustrates how paying attention to even seemingly minor details can make a major difference. And as a physician, I know only too well the truism that "an ounce of prevention is worth a pound of cure." If more people would practice preventive medicine, many doctors would be out of business.

Disasters disrupt hundreds of thousands of lives every year. Living in the mountains of western North Carolina, my wife and I have personally experienced electrical outages four times in the last eight years due to ice storms. One such storm left us without power for four days. Good thing we had a contingency plan and some good neighbors, who opened their home, kept our frozen foods cold and warmed our hearts.

On another occasion, I learned the hard way about the need to make sure my phones, computers, and fax machine had surge protectors. That was an expensive lesson.

If disaster preparedness is a "no-brainer," then why are many, if not most, unprepared or only minimally prepared when calamity strikes? Are only simpletons not "watching ahead?" No! Then "Why?"

BARRIERS TO PREPAREDNESS

There are many reasons for failing to prepare for the future. I would like to say the "reasons" are just "excuses" and that may be true in part. As a physician, however, I have observed extreme levels of stress and burnout in our society, that make it almost impossible for some people to think clearly, never mind thinking ahead.

With the high percentage of single-parent families and the need for two wage earners to make ends meet in other families, there is barely enough time to take care of the absolute necessities, much less anything added to the agenda. I also see segments of our society alienated from the mainstream, young people who are pessimistic about the future and fatalistic toward what is coming to pass on the earth. These are significant barriers to disaster preparedness.

This mindset is not unique to the United States. Having served in 105 nations, I see the same patterns of fear, uncertainty and stress everywhere I go.

Yet this picture does not have to be true. For those of us who believe in Jesus, we can prepare for the worst with serenity. I once heard of an artist who was commissioned to paint a portrait of peace. Rather than painting some idyllic pastoral scene, he chose to depict a fierce storm beating against the craggy face of a mountain. Tucked safely in a cleft of the rock was a nest. In the nest was a little bird, her head thrown back. She was singing at the top of her lungs. The storm raged all around her, but she knew she was safe.

IMPACT OF WORLDVIEW ON PREPAREDNESS

Your worldview has much to say about "why" or "if" you prepare for disasters. Your worldview begins at home with how you respond to the needs of your own family, your next-door neighbor, and your community.

As I mentioned in the introduction, 80-90 percent of all Americans have not made adequate preparations for disasters. That's where *you* come in. It is important for Christians to know that significant segments of society will not be ready for crises, but will need assistance when disasters do occur. This lack of foresight will impact the resources of those who are prepared. If you are among the 80-90 percent not ready for an emergency, join the ranks of the 10-20 percent who are. Rather than producing fear, knowledge of what to expect and how to prepare ahead of time should encourage Christians to use these wide doors of opportunity for the church to reach out to others with compassionate care in times of crisis.

Christians and the church also need to be prepared to help those who traditionally reject them and who hold widely disparate worldviews, both within our nation and internationally. It is important that we understand these views in order to minister to the people who hold a different worldview.

Significant segments of our society will not respond readily to the call for preparedness due to their pessimism about the future. Many are nihilistic, cynical, feel alienated, and mistrust traditional values. It is important for believers to come to grips with the fact that major segments of our nation's young people are indifferent toward religion and may reject and even take a hostile stance toward the religion of their parents. Many do, in fact, believe in God or at least a "higher power" and are accepting the plurality of world religions.

Those holding these views present a special challenge to the church and to those of us who are making the calls to prepare for storms that may lie ahead. The prophetic teachings of the Bible are often rejected and the teachings of many Christians are just another instance of crying, "Wolf!"

Another worldview that greatly impacts one's preparation for disasters is found among those religions of the world that hold fatalistic views of world events. I have even heard some Christians say, "We can do nothing about what is happening, so why prepare?" Some Christians believe that they will be taken out of the world before the major tragedies of the Tribulation period spoken of in the prophetic Scriptures and, therefore, do not believe they need to prepare for major disasters.

Let me give you an international example of working among other peoples who hold a fatalistic worldview. In December, 2004, an earthquake hit just off the coast of Banda Aceh, Indonesia, resulting in tsunamis that affected many different nations and left hundreds of thousands dead, the highest toll being in Banda Aceh.

Banda Aceh, known as the "Porch of Islam," is under Sharia Muslim law. Interestingly enough, other than local national governmental responses, it was notably countries with historic Judeo-Christian roots that sent volunteers to help with the multiple disasters. The majority of non-governmental organizations that responded were also Christian.

Three weeks after the tsunami hit, I networked several organizations and led a medical team to Banda Aceh. Bringing a large amount of medications and supplies with us and working in over five different sites, we were able to make a significant impact. The patients were extremely grateful.

My response to disasters, however, is not determined by whether or not someone appreciates what I am doing or understands my motives. I believe I have a biblical mandate to respond with Christ's compassion. My admonition to you is that when you see the naked or those who are cold and hungry, do not just say, "God bless you." Rather, give them the practical material things they need, just as you would want someone to do for you.

PRESSURES TO "JUST GET BY"

Most failures to prepare for disasters are rooted in the fact that many people are struggling just to keep their heads above water financially and juggling day-to-day responsibilities. There seems to be no time. When time is available, it is used to relax or relieve tensions, not take on more responsibility.

Looking into the faces of people, I see the heavy loads they carry—for example, a young single woman struggling with two small children, a baby in her arms and a toddler tugging at her jeans. I see the burdens of the world weighing her down.

I think of the country/pop song written by Hank Cochran and popularized by Eddy Arnold, "Make The World Go Away." It hit the number-one spot in 1965. It is still a classic today.

The song speaks of love gone by the wayside; hope and intimacy seemingly gone forever. Reading the lyrics again makes me want to reach out and help the young woman whom I picture in my mind as abused and abandoned, jilted by an unfaithful lover. Somehow I want to extend hope to her by making it as easy as possible to prepare for even more difficult times.

I also want to challenge the church (see Chapter 8) and the transformers within the church (see Chapter 9) to pick up the slack when she cannot do it on her own. She needs help *now,* not just in times of disaster.

THE LEAST OF THESE

Of the ten worst natural disasters in the twentieth century, measured in terms of loss of human life, seven occurred in Bangladesh. One of the poorest nations on earth, Bangladesh has the highest population density and a fertile delta that floods frequently. The geography of the Bay of Bengal is such, that when cyclones form off the coast of Bangladesh and head toward land, huge tidal waves are created, killing thousands of people each time.

In the early 1990s, 130,000 people perished from a cyclone, including 40,000 people on the island of Katubdia when a 20-foot wall of water washed over it. Three weeks after the cyclone hit, I led a medical team, the first relief workers to reach the island. We were helicoptered in by the U.S. military to establish a "hospital" in one of the few buildings left standing. Our team treated several thousand people, many with cholera.

Despite the severity of this international tragedy, it received very little attention from the world community. Yet, because the highest point on the island is only ten feet above sea level, this kind of disaster will happen again and again. Apparently, though, since developed nations have no vested interests in this region, no effective strategies have been put in place to minimize the damage. And like the single mother of the illustration used earlier, Bangladesh cannot take care of herself.

Where is the conscience of the world community? Others know of the great dangers to this entire people group. Thousands of lives could be saved in Bangladesh if international financing and planning were set in motion.

What about "the least of these" in the city or countryside where you live? Planning ahead will make a huge difference in their lives as well as your own. America is usually quick to respond to disasters. May we never lose our national conscience!

It is interesting to note that despite the vast resources available in the United States, 85 pecent or more of its citizens are not prepared for most disasters, even the more common ones. I challenge you to be among those who *are* prepared.

PART TWO

WHAT YOU NEED TO PREPARE FOR

COMMON THINGS HAPPEN COMMONLY

"When you hear hoof beats behind you, do you think of horses or zebras?"

The answer is, of course, "Horses."

"Common things happen commonly."

CHAPTER 3

HORSES OR ZEBRAS?
WHAT TO PREPARE FOR

I attended medical school at Washington University School of Medicine, St. Louis, Missouri. Washington University is a major referral center, and many people with very unusual and rare diseases and medical conditions go there for diagnosis and treatment.

During my medical training, my professors taught me how to diagnose various diseases. When faced with a difficult case, I was advised to think first of what was most common and consider that diagnosis.

They would ask, "When you hear hoof beats behind you, do you think of horses or zebras?" The answer is, of course, "Horses." The only problem at Washington University was that I often saw more medical "zebras" than horses. It was only after I graduated and entered a more typical medical practice that I learned, experientially, the truism that "common things happen commonly."

Now take this statement and apply it to disaster preparedness. What are the common emergencies you can anticipate facing? Depending upon where you live, are you most likely to face tornadoes, hurricanes, flooding, ice storms, fires, electrical storms, extreme heat, extreme cold, or earthquakes? Plan for what is most likely to occur in your area. Look for the horses, not the zebras.

As for me, living in the mountains, my wife and I have experienced ice storms, power outages, and occasional flooding. So those are the kinds of emergencies I focus on. If I am prepared for what I can reasonably expect to happen, I will be better prepared should a zebra show up.

Special plans must be made for those in your family who require special assistance, such as the elderly, the handicapped, or the chronically ill. For example, I recently heard of a family whose son was on a respirator and needed a generator during a power failure. A request for help went out over a local radio station and the need was met. But it would have made things easier for this family if they had already acquired a back-up generator for such emergencies.

BASIC PREPAREDNESS

Some basic principles apply to most emergencies. In fact, if you plan ahead for what I call "normal contingencies," you will often find yourself taking the same steps you would take if preparing for a disaster.

1. Physical Fitness and Good Nutrition are foundational to any disaster preparedness plan. The problem of obesity is acknowledged as a major health issue in America and makes a person vulnerable in times of crisis. Check out the website *www. exrx.net* for instructions on calisthenics, nutrition, and weight training. Many other good resources are available. It is now up to you to put the advice into action.

2. First Aid and Basic Life Support Courses are also very important. Check with your local Red Cross agency or YMCA facility for a schedule of classes. The life you save may be your own or that of a family member.

3. Disaster Preparedness Resources are available through the Department of Homeland Security.

(See Appendix A for an additional list of excellent disaster preparedness books and resources.)

FIRST STEPS

If you have never really sat down and applied yourself to finding out what to do or where to go for emergency preparedness information, spend several hours some weekend and learn the basics presented in this chapter.

Make a list of action steps. Add to or tailor the steps to your specific situation. Be sure to prioritize the steps, and then set aside at least an hour or two each week to work on them. Taking your action steps in smaller bites is more realistic and will fit more easily into your budget. Don't wait for the "big day" when you plan to get it all done. Also, by knowing what needs to be done and what may yet need to be purchased, you can pick up a number of these items over time on regular shopping days.

Learn about your local community's plans for warning and evacuation. Contact the emergency management office of your local chapter of the American Red Cross. City, county and state offices, fire and rescue stations and the police and sheriffs' offices all have information on disaster preparedness. Keeping the phone numbers and location of these offices handy may prove crucial in times of disaster.

I have formatted this chapter to function as a "workbook." Read the following questions and recommendations and indicate your response. If the question or recommendation has already been completed, mark it off the list. The remaining items will become your action list. Be sure to prioritize.

THE HORSES: HAZARDS TO PREPARE FOR

What hazards and emergencies are you most likely to face in your community?

Circle all that apply and then rank them according to risk level: High, Moderate, or Low. Suggestion: Don't just rely on your own knowledge, but ask local authorities as well, particularly if you have not lived very long in your present location. As an example, to my surprise, I learned that earthquakes are a natural hazard where I live.

Natural Hazards	Risk Level		
Floods	H	M	L
Hurricanes	H	M	L
Thunderstorms/lightning	H	M	L
Tornadoes	H	M	L
Winter storms/ice storms	H	M	L
Extreme Cold	H	M	L
Extreme Heat	H	M	L
Earthquakes	H	M	L
Fires	H	M	L
Wildfires	H	M	L
Landslides and debris flow	H	M	L
Volcanoes	H	M	L
Tsunamis	H	M	L

Technological Hazards			
Hazardous materials incidents	H	M	L
Nuclear power plants	H	M	L

Once you have determined what is more likely to occur in the area in which you live, obtain the preparedness guidelines for those hazards and share this information with your family and neighbors.

(See Appendix A for common preparedness guidelines and additional list of excellent disaster preparedness books and resources.)

Mark the appropriate response for each hazard you circled above.

Write the hazard name in the blank space and then circle **Yes** or No. Make a separate copy for each hazard you circled:

I know how to respond to _____   Yes   No

I have a hard copy of how to prepare.   Yes   No

I have shared this information with my family. Yes   No

I have made the recommended preparations.   Yes   No

Once you have marked the responses for each anticipated hazard, make a list of the Nos. You have just generated your Action Items.

ACTION ITEMS

- Keep a hard copy for frequent review. (See Chapter 11.)

- Place this information where everyone in the family can find it easily!

- **Do not rely on having access to the Internet to get last-minute information.** Remember, phone and Internet communication and even satellite phone communication may not be available following some disasters.

What emergency warning systems are available in your community?

The *Emergency Alert System* (EAS) can address the entire nation on very short notice in case of national emergencies.

National Oceanic & Atmospheric Administration (NOAA) *and National Weather Radio* (NWR) is a nationwide network of radio stations broadcasting continuous information directly from a nearby National Weather Service office to specially configured NOAA weather radio receivers.

WARNING SYSTEMS

Emergency Alert System	Yes	No
NOAA Weather Radio	Yes	No
Local TV participates in the EAS.	Yes	No
Local radio stations participate in the EAS.	Yes	No

If you don't know the answers, find out. Also, list any other warning systems used in your local area such as sirens to warn of tornadoes, etc. In some areas a pre-planned phone list system has been put in place to notify neighbors when disasters are imminent. Ask your local authorities about any other methods used to warn your community.

If you are in an area where weather disturbances are a significant risk, consider purchasing a NOAA weather radio receiver if the NOAA Weather Radio is available. This could even be a neighborhood action item.

During the time we have been living in North Carolina, we have experienced severe flooding and loss of electrical power. Once, for several days, my wife and I received our primary information from an emergency radio broadcast by a local Baptist minister, who coordinated special needs over the radio including the need of the young man for a generator to power his ventilator. During certain times of the night this radio broadcast was the only emergency information available.

WHEN EVACUATION BECOMES NECESSARY

Evacuations are more common than you might think. Flooding, hurricanes, fires, and industrial accidents are among the reasons people must be evacuated from an area.

I remember flying into Miami just before the airport was closed as

Hurricane Andrew was bearing down on the region. All north and south lanes of the major interstate highways were filled with traffic heading north. I recall the strange feeling driving north on a south-bound lane, bumper-to-bumper in the pouring rain!

It happened again on September 11, 2001. My wife and I were to attend a banquet in Washington, D.C. that night. We tried to get into D.C., but all lanes of traffic across the Potomac River were "heading out of Dodge!" We did manage to make it into the city by detouring through Maryland. It was a weird feeling.

More recently, we all watched the incredible traffic tie-ups as people fled New Orleans with Hurricane Katrina bearing down.

Whether planning evacuation routes for local flooding, or getting out of the way of a hurricane or in response to an act of terror, it is important to make plans should an emergency occur that requires you to evacuate your home or community.

In the event that you and your family must be evacuated from your home or other locations, mark the following:

I know the emergency evacuation routes for my community determined by local authorities.	Yes	No
I have a copy of a map with evacuation routes clearly marked.	Yes	No
I have made an evacuation plan for myself and my family (may be different from one above).	Yes	No
I have planned where to meet family should we be in separate areas when a disaster hits.	Yes	No

General guidelines for evacuation in the DHS/FEMA publication "Are You Ready?"[1] include:

- Keep a full tank of gas in your car if an evacuation seems likely. Gas stations may be closed during emergencies and unable to pump gas during power outages.

- Plan to take one car per family to reduce congestion and delay. (I would add that a single vehicle also simplifies matters should you have to take detours; one car also avoids the possibility of becoming separated.)

- Make transportation arrangements with friends or local government if you do not own a car.

- Listen to battery-powered radio and follow local evacuation instructions.

- Gather your family and go if you are instructed to evacuate immediately.

- Leave early enough to avoid being trapped by severe weather.

- Follow recommended evacuation routes. Do not take shortcuts; they may be blocked. Note: Be sure to listen to local disaster instructions by radio or TV, if available, in case the community-planned evacuation route has had to be altered for any reason.

- Be alert for washed-out roads and bridges. Do not drive into flooded areas.

- Stay away from downed power lines.

Further instructions are given if time permits:

- Gather your disaster supplies kit. (I would add that this is not an option, assuming it is just a matter of grabbing the kit and if there is room in the vehicle. I recommend that the kit be in a soft-sided, duffle-bag type container or backpack.)

- Wear sturdy shoes and clothing that provides some protection, such as long pants, long-sleeved shirts, and a cap.

- Secure your home.

  - Close and lock doors and windows.

  - Unplug electrical equipment, such as radios, televisions, and small appliances. Leave freezers and refrigerators plugged unless there is a risk of flooding.

- For some emergencies it may be necessary to shut off gas, electricity and water utilities.

- Let others know where you are or will be going.

This last point is a major one! Few situations are more anxiety-producing than knowing a loved one is facing an emergency or disaster and you do not know how to get in touch. Sometimes phone communication is impossible. In such cases, leave notes or attempt to contact authorities.

COMMUNITY DISASTER PLANS

In July, 2006, the United States Conference of Mayors released a major emergency preparedness/homeland security survey that showed that only 73 percent of the cities with populations over 300,000 had recently created or updated an evacuation plan; only 56 percent of all cities had done so. That means 44 percent of all cities in the United States have not created or updated their evacuation plans.

Most disaster preparedness documents provide summaries to give you enough details about the things you should know as a local citizen. For the expected "horse" emergencies, a great majority of the local and regional plans are adequate, although you will want to find out if the document has been updated recently.

The following items relate to your local community disaster response plans:

My community has a disaster response plan.   Yes   No

If yes, do you have a copy?   Yes   No

Has this plan been updated recently?   Yes   No

HURRICANE KATRINA

The magnitude of Hurricane Katrina, coupled with flooding, made Katrina one of the greatest natural disasters in our history. The local community and state disaster plans were overwhelmed. The area is still reeling from the after-effects.

With many hospitals and clinic facilities destroyed, major health challenges faced the region, post-Katrina. *USA Today* claimed deaths were up 47 percent in New Orleans due to decreased availability and access to adequate healthcare.

For major catastrophic events such as Katrina, we still have serious gaps in preparedness as a nation, particularly at state and local levels. The National Response Plan (NRP) and National Incident Management System (NIMS) have made significant attempts to correct these deficiencies, but most state and local plans have not adequately addressed issues such as bioterrorism, bird-flu pandemic, mass casualties, healthcare personnel shortages, and health issues for the uninsured during times of emergencies. At the heart of many of the deficiencies is the question, "Where is the money to fund all the solutions?"

There are major issues of community preparedness to handle evacuees and the need to develop partnerships with private industry. Even in my home state of North Carolina, hundreds of victims of Hurricane Katrina were housed for a period of time while reconstruction was underway.

The tragedy of Katrina emphasizes the need for personal preparedness, which is the primary thrust of this book.

SCHOOL EMERGENCY PLAN

Another area of emergency planning where you must be proactive is your children's school emergency plan. If you have not already done so, take personal responsibility for learning the plan. Every school is required to have one. Each school is also expected, on a regular basis, to instruct the students in drills for such emergencies as fire and tornadoes.

Mark the following items related to your children's school emergency plan:

I know my children's school emergency plan.   Yes No

I have received a copy from each school (if   Yes No
more than one, including day-care).

I know how each school will communicate Yes No
with families when a crisis occurs.

Does each school have adequate food, water and basic supplies should a crisis develop?	Yes	No
I know the school is prepared to shelter the students onsite, if necessary.	Yes	No
I know where the school plans to evacuate the children, if necessary.	Yes	No
I have done similar planning with babysitters and/or daycare facilities.	Yes	No
I have stored this information, along with other preparedness documents, in a prominent location in my home.	Yes	No

If, for whatever reason, you suspect that the "normal" routine of responding to emergencies or disasters may not work out, contingency arrangements with other family members and/or neighbors and friends should be in place ahead of time. Schools will not release children to anyone who is not on an approved list.

I have arranged for a friend or neighbor to pick up my children from school in case I am unable to do so. The name is on the approved school list.	Yes	No

U.S DEPARTMENT OF EDUCATION INFORMATION

For more information on developing emergency preparedness plans for schools, log on to the U. S. Department of Education at *www. ed.gov/emergencyplan.*

WORKPLACE PLANS

Mark the following items related to disaster planning in your workplace:

My workplace has a written disaster plan.	Yes	No
I have a copy.	Yes	No
My workplace has a building evacuation plan.	Yes	No
The building evacuation plan is regularly practiced.	Yes	No
The heating, ventilation and air conditioning systems are secure and have good filtering.	Yes	No
I know how to turn off critical electric equipment (such as air conditioning) if needed.	Yes	No
My workplace has a first aid kit that is updated regularly and has good-date medications and supplies.	Yes	No
My workplace has a portable, battery-operated radio and extra batteries.	Yes	No
My workplace has hard hats and masks for dust.	Yes	No

My guess is that many smaller businesses do not have many of the items listed above. If not, take the initiative and help your office prepare for emergencies.

HERE COME THE ZEBRAS!
PREPARING FOR TERRORIST ATTACKS

Acts of terrorism, of course, are almost impossible for the ordinary citizen to predict, but certain precautions can be taken. Some general recommendations are given by the DHS/FEMA publication, "Are You Ready?" The publication covers explosions, biological threats, chemical threats, nuclear blast, radiological dispersion device (dirty bomb) and the Homeland Security Advisory System. This is an easy-to-read, quick resource for terrorism preparedness. (See Appendix A for more in-depth resources on this topic.)

The following includes information adapted from the DHS/FEMA recommendations, interspersed with my comments and thoughts.

High-risk targets for acts of terrorism include:

- military and civilian government facilities
- international airports
- large cities
- high-profile landmarks

You will have to determine if you fit into a low-, medium-, or high-risk profile and take steps to inform yourself about those areas for which you are at greatest risk. This is beyond the scope of this book. If, however, you are prepared for the "Horses," you will be better prepared for the "Zebras."

In preparing for terrorist acts, we must also consider transportation. I am a frequent flyer—often traveling in and out of international airports. In fact, while writing this book, I am scheduled to go to India and Cambodia through Atlanta and JFK airports. A terrorist plot at JFK—the very airport I will be flying out of—was exposed in the past few months. So what do I do? Do I cancel my travel plans? Do I give in to fear? No! I do, however, take precautions:

- I pay attention more closely to what is going on around me.
- I try to be aware of any unusual behavior.
- I do not accept packages from strangers.
- I do not leave my luggage unattended.

How should Christians respond to terrorist threats in our volatile environment? Let me share a experience I faced before 9-11 that will perhaps illustrate how the Lord protects and guides us by His Spirit when we face potentially dangerous situations.

Several years ago I took a medical team to Barranquilla, Columbia, South America. A few weeks prior to our leaving, an explosion occurred in Bogotá that killed about eighty people associated with the government (in a branch similar to our FBI).

Our team was scheduled to fly on Avianca Airlines. Just a few days before leaving the U.S., an Avianca plane was blown up flying out of Bogotá, Columbia. It was alleged that the drug cartel had something to do with the incident. Then just a day or so before leaving, there was the rumor of a bomb aboard another Avianca flight out of Los Angeles. This one proved to be a false alarm.

At this point, one of my team members cancelled, saying her parents did not want her to take the risk. I understood. I began praying earnestly! I told the Lord I didn't mind dying for the Gospel and for my faith, but I didn't want to die for some drug cartel! The responsibility of taking a team into a place of potential danger weighed heavily on me.

When the chaplain of our team, Jose Garrastegui, and I prayed together, we sensed in our spirits that there would be danger in Barranquilla, but that it was OK to take the team.

As it turned out, we did have a man come to our last day of clinic at the church with a gun and every intention of shooting us. Others came with the intent of stealing medications, but their plans were thwarted. None of the evil that had been planned took place.

Instead, the man who came in with a shoulder holster, prayed with us to receive Christ into his life! I had been unaware of what was going on, but was told later that he had been standing only ten feet from me as I was speaking to the crowd about the love of Jesus before we left the church.

The protection of the Lord and the guidance of His Spirit are gifts God makes available to all believers. Use these gifts to bless yourself, your family and community!

Now, retrace your steps and list the action items you have identified in this chapter. Get ready to add these action items to the lists you will create in the next chapter, "Ready Or Not?"

HIDE-AND-GO-SEEK

As a kid I enjoyed playing "Hide-and-Go-Seek." If I were "It," meaning the one to find everyone else, I'd close my eyes while the others hid, count to one hundred, and yell at the top of my lungs, "Ready or not, here I come!"

There would always be some younger playmate who hadn't caught on to the art of concealment. When I saw him moving behind a curtain—if the game were played inside—or rustling the shrubbery—if outside—I would know exactly where he was hiding. In no time at all, I had tagged him and he was "It!" Sometimes, in case of a much younger child, I'd let him off the hook and go in search of more difficult prey.

It was loads of fun! It was just a game. The kids who were not prepared or didn't know where to hide risked nothing more than being caught and having to be "It."

Ironically, times of disaster bring situations of hide-and-go-seek. But life is not a game. When trouble comes, we must be ready…spiritually and physically.

CHAPTER 4

READY OR NOT?
CHECKLISTS AND FOLLOW-UP

Several years ago my wife Sofia and I went to Israel for one month to work with Barry and Batya Segal and Joseph's Storehouse. While there, we visited a number of sites where the Israelis had pre-positioned medical supplies in anticipation of future conflicts in those areas, such as Hebron. One of the Israeli soldiers pointed to a room in the café where we were eating and said matter-of-factly, "That room over there has been designated as the surgical room, if necessary."

The Israelis understand the need for preparedness. Each Israeli family makes up emergency backpacks for every member and places the packs in a readily accessible place in their homes, cars, and workplace. The backpacks at home include passports or identification documents, money, and an assortment of supplies for at least three days' survival. The criteria for what one can take are that the supplies must fit into one backpack per person. It amazed me what they were able to get into one backpack!

We would do well to follow their example.

EMERGENCY SUPPLIES KITS

At least three different emergency supplies kits are generally recommended for each household—one kit for the home, one for the car, and one for the workplace. I have chosen to name these kits Emergency Supplies Kits rather than Disaster Supplies Kits to make the point that all emergencies do not qualify as disasters and that we should be ready for any adversity.

In addition to having a Grab-and-Go bag at home, in the car, and in the office, Anton Edwards, in *Preparedness Now!,* suggests that a person carry an emergency supplies kit at all times. He advocates the use of a sturdy pouch worn on a strong belt or placed in your purse, briefcase, or backpack. Although you may not feel the need for this extreme measure, you should definitely consider it seriously if you work in a tall building in an urban setting, live in a high-rise, or frequently use public transportation, such as subways.

HOME EMERGENCY "GRAB-and-GO-BAG" SUPPLIES KIT

I recommend that the emergency supplies for the home be handled as follows: Fill a container with emergency supplies that will fit into the trunk of a car or in the back of SUV or pickup, in case evacuation is necessary. That's why we call it a "Grab-and-Go-bag."

Select a high-quality backpack, preferably waterproof (otherwise you will need to obtain a backpack cover). Be sure you are able to readily carry whatever you place in the backpack in case you are forced to evacuate your home on foot.

INDIVIDUAL FAMILY MEMBER
EMERGENCY PACKS

In addition, be sure each individual family member packs his or her own smaller or medium-sized backpack with individual supplies that may be unique to them such as clothing, medications, etc. The size I saw the Israelis use was only the size of a child's school backpack. Larger backpacks may be used if each family member can readily carry the weight.

If family members have to separate, each has his or her own pack and there will be no loss of time in dividing up the supplies. Also, if evacuation needs to be on foot, everyone is ready to go!

ADDITIONAL EMERGENCY SUPPLIES
FOR EXTENDED PERIODS

Making up Emergency Supplies Kits does not represent adequate preparedness for your home. In addition to the kits, I will be addressing the preparations that should be made at your home in the event you are able to remain there. You may be isolated for an extended period of time because of prolonged flooding or power outages.

Keep a minimum of 14 days of food supplies and drinking water in the home. Water filtration systems and water purification chemicals will greatly extend your safe water supply availability. Many disaster preparation advocates encourage people to have a 3 to 6 months' supply of food. This recommendation becomes a significant economic factor for many households and many will not be able to do so, even if desired. (See Appendix B.)

Below I have listed some of the recommended items to place in each emergency supplies kit. Just check off each item when you have added it to your kit. Make assembling your emergency kit into a game to include younger children. Do not make preparation fearful.

PERISHABLE GOODS AND ITEMS WITH EXPIRATION DATES

Keep a list of perishable items or those with expiration dates along with your other emergency documents. Develop some type of alert system to remind yourself when these items should be replaced. This can be easily done on a computer, or place the list in a folder for review on a regular schedule.

In their book, *Crisis Evangelism*, Drs. Mark and Betsy Neuenschwander state: "A simple way to achieve long-term food storage without breaking the budget is summed up in the phrase '*Store what you eat, and eat what you store.*'"

When shopping for items you normally use, purchase and store several extra items. Develop a rotation system for using the older items first. This will allow you to gradually build up your food storage.

Another approach is to buy food in bulk for long-term storage. (See Appendix B.) For additional guidance as to what to have on hand, go to *www.ready.gov.* You may also consult *Don't Get Caught with Your Pantry Down,* by James T. Stevens (Austin: Historical Publications, 1998).

CHECKLIST FOR HOME EMERGENCY SUPPLIES KIT
HOME "GRAB-and-GO-BAG"
(Appendix C)

Essential food (minimum 3 days) _____
(Many recommend up to 2 weeks' food supply.)

Special dietary foods (if needed) _____

Water (1 gal./person/day; minimum 3 days) _____

Portable water filtration system _____
(Many smaller camping devices work well, but

more sophisticated systems are available
if affordable. Remember to consider bulkiness.)

Water purification tablets or solution   _____
(Be sure to follow instructions carefully.)

Portable, battery-powered radio or TV   _____
with extra batteries
(Hand-rechargeable radios are also good.)

Flashlights and extra batteries   _____
 (Flashlights that don't require batteries
prevent the need for fresh batteries. Solar-
powered lights are available; also solar-powered
recharging units for AA, AAA, B, C, D batteries.)

First aid kit and manual   _____
(Kit needs to be periodically updated for
items with expiration dates. List of recommended
items is provided in chapter 7 and Appendix D.)

Insect repellent (mosquito netting)   _____

Smoke hoods (especially if living in high-rise   _____
or multi-storied buildings)

Crowbar (small)   _____

Roll of duct tape (flattened)   _____

Nylon cord (550-lb. test)   _____

Sanitation and hygiene items   _____
(moist towelettes, toilet paper, sanitary napkins)

Waterproof matches or matches in a waterproof   _____
container

Lighters   _____

Heavy-duty plastic garbage bags   _____

Kitchen accessories and cooking utensils
including a manual can opener
(Camping cookware may work well.)

    _____

Whistle

    _____

Signal flare

    _____

Small tool kit (wrench, pliers, other tools)
(Or use a multi-tool, e.g., Kershaw locking pliers
or Leatherman Crunch.)

    _____

Scissors (preferably EMT scissors, also called
bandage scissors)

    _____

Needle and thread (sewing kit)

    _____

Extra set of house keys and car keys

    _____

Plastic sheeting
(This is particularly useful for sheltering
family or personal goods from rain, etc.)

    _____

Medium-sized plastic bucket with tight lid

    _____

Disinfectant and household chlorine bleach

    _____

Small shovel (for digging a latrine)
(Foldable camping shovel works fine.)

    _____

Small canister, ABC-type fire extinguisher

    _____

Tube tent

    _____

Compass

    _____

Work gloves

    _____

Extra clothing
(Recommended clothing will vary according
to where you live and weather you anticipate

    _____

if evacuation is required.)

Rain gear   _____

Prescription medications   _____
(Rotate regularly so medications do not
become outdated. Check with your doctor
ahead of time to determine if a medication
is safe to use after the expiration date.)

Eye glasses, contact lens solutions   _____
(Be sure to renew regularly.)

Goggles for emergency eye protection   _____
(Can use simple swimming goggles.)

Hearing aid batteries (if applicable)   _____

Items for infants (formula, diapers, bottles   _____
pacifiers, etc.)
(This is a good time to encourage breast
feeding! Saves on storage requirements!
Make sure formula is renewed regularly.)

Emergency contact list and phone numbers   _____
(Include police, fire, doctor, hospital, schools,
electric, gas, water companies; place list next to
phone in the home as well as in emergency grab-
and-go bag.)

Family emergency contact list and phone   _____
numbers
(Include out-of-area family and E-mail
addresses in case Internet access should
not become available. Include pictures of
each family member. Store in waterproof
container.)

Map of local area and/or places where you   _____
might go if evacuating
(Store in waterproof container.)

Photocopies of credit and identification cards   _____
(Store in plastic or waterproof container.)

Copies of important documents in waterproof   _____
container such as insurance and vital records
(See Appendix E for more complete list.)

Cash and some coins (watertight container)   _____
(Obtain at least $500 in small bills; some
recommend up to $3,000. You cannot be
guaranteed access to ATMs or bank
accounts, and small bills will make it easier in
paying for any services or goods.)

Paper, pens, pencils (waterproof container)   _____
(Waterproof notebooks may be found at sporting
goods stores.)

Everyone in the family should know where   _____
the emergency kit is located.

For those living in a cold climate, add the following items to your emergency supplies kit.

Jacket/coat (the least bulky that will provide   _____
adequate warmth)

Long pants, long-sleeved shirt   _____

Sturdy shoes like hiking boots   _____

Hat/head covering/gloves/scarf   _____

Sleeping bag or blanket (per person)   _____

     The above list of emergency supplies should be placed in one or two easy-to-carry containers such as backpacks or duffel bags.

     My personal recommendation is to take care of the basic emergency preparations, pray about any additional steps you might take, and do what feels best to you.

"GRAB-and-GO BAG" STORAGE

Store your Grab-and-Go bag(s) where you have rapid and easy access. In times of extreme emergency, you may not have much time to find them. Store bags away from high-risk areas such as the kitchen, where fires are a greater potential risk.

Check the weight of your bag. A good rule of thumb is not to pack more than one-fourth of your body weight unless you are in good shape physically.

CAR EMERGENCY SUPPLIES

Now let's consider what should be carried in the car, SUV, or whatever vehicle will most likely be used in an emergency.

Outfit each vehicle with such universally necessary items as jumper cables, flares, and first aid supplies, but keep a more complete emergency supplies kit in the vehicle you would most likely use if evacuation becomes necessary.

CHECKLIST FOR CAR EMERGENCY SUPPLIES

Jumper cables   _____

Flares   _____

Flat tire inflation canister (non-explosive)   _____

Spare tire and jack   _____

First aid supplies   _____

Water (several gallons)
(Frequently replenish supply.)   _____

High-energy foods/power bars   _____

Small tool kit   _____

Flashlight/batteries/flashlight   _____

that does not need batteries

Road maps   _____
(Consider hand-held GPS device if your car
does not have a GPS.)

Blankets   _____

Seasonal supplies (such as umbrellas)   _____

Several disaster preparedness manuals provide a more extensive
list of recommended items for car emergency supplies. Review Appendix
F and determine if you want to add to the above list. If you live in an
area where evacuation occasionally has been ordered, such as the Carolina
coast, a more extensive stocking of your vehicle may be in order.

WORKPLACE EMERGENCY SUPPLIES KIT

I keep a personal first aid kit at work. (See Appendix G.)	Yes	No
I keep several days' supply of needed prescription medications at work and rotate monthly.	Yes	No
I keep comfortable walking shoes or boots at my workplace, in case evacuation is necessary.	Yes	No
I keep emergency food and water available at work.	Yes	No
Flashlight (type that does not require batteries)	Yes	No
Small emergency radio	Yes	No
Mini-pry bar	Yes	No
Smoke hood, in case of fire	Yes	No

Extra keys (home and vehicles)	Yes	No
Duct tape	Yes	No
Nylon cord (550-lb. test, if you work in multi-story building)	Yes	No
I have these emergency workplace items in a readily accessible "Grab-and-Go" bag.	Yes	No

MAINTAINING YOUR EMERGENCY SUPPLIES KITS

It is important to maintain your emergency kits, particularly the food, first aid kits, and medications. Also, periodically review your situation and determine if you need to modify what you are keeping in your kits.

Regarding food, I recommend you rotate new supplies on a monthly basis for those items that do not have an indefinite shelf life. Place a card or note with the food, noting the date you need to rotate your food stock.

Keep a content list with the kits of all the items included in your emergency kits. Highlight the dates when you need to update the medications and supplies in the first aid kits.

SPECIAL HANDLING OF MEDICATIONS AND FIRST AID KITS

An important safety measure used by professional emergency teams is to seal medications and first aid containers and label them, showing the date the contents need to be updated. When the seal is broken (you may use tape, wire, or string), you will know that the contents need to be reviewed and any missing items replaced. You will also know that if the seal is intact, the right supplies are in the bag.

Try **not** to use these supplies for "routine" minor emergencies like scraped knees or cuts. Have a separate first aid kit for normal household use. This will keep your true emergency kit ready for the real emergencies.

CHECKLIST FOR MAINTAINING
EMERGENCY KITS

I have made a content list of each emergency kit.　　Yes　　No

I have placed a note with the food as to when I　　Yes　　No
need to rotate in new stock.

I have highlighted the dates that medications and　　Yes　　No
first aid supplies need to be updated.

I have sealed my medication containers and first　　Yes　　No
aid kits, noting the dates I need to update contents.

LEARNING FIRST AID AND CPR

The Red Cross and many hospital and health clinics offer First Aid and CPR training. Official certification by the Red Cross is available; under "Good Samaritan" laws, you will be protected if you administer first aid in an emergency.

ADDITIONAL EMERGENCY PLANNING - FIRE!

Our oldest son and his family experienced a power outage during a major winter storm in Indiana. Using a generator loaned by some friends to keep the furnace going, my son assumed there was adequate ventilation in the garage. Unfortunately, this was not the case.

In the middle of the night an alarm went off and a verbal warning sounded, indicating that the carbon monoxide levels were dangerously high. Our son and his wife evacuated our three grandchildren, who were sleeping upstairs. When the fire rescue squad arrived, they judged the levels to be lethal in the area where the children had been!

Our daughter-in-law had just recently purchased the smoke detector that was also capable of detecting carbon monoxide. When my wife and I heard the story, you can imagine the incredible relief we felt and the thanksgiving we gave to the Lord for His protection!

In the case of a house fire, there is much you can do to minimize the damage to life and property if you will plan ahead.

SMOKE AND CARBON MONOXIDE DECTECTORS

Fires starting inside the home as opposed to fires originating from outside the home are a universal risk. To prepare for such events, smoke detectors are a must. In fact, you can't get insurance on your home or apartments without them. Battery-operated smoke detectors are preferred over those dependent upon electricity because of the likelihood of power outages. Some smoke detectors—as our family learned—also detect carbon monoxide.

ESCAPE LADDERS

If you have two or more stories in your home or apartment, consider the possible need for an emergency escape ladder. Find out what type of ladder is best suited for your living quarters. Even in a high-rise building, a ladder may allow you to escape to a lower floor.

FIRE EXTINGUISHERS

Secure at least one fire extinguisher of the ABC type. Teach your family members how to use it and be sure everyone knows where it is.

PLAN TWO ESCAPE ROUTES

Draw a floor plan of your home and mark two routes of escape from each room. Post a copy of these plans in each child's room at eye level. Practice the escape routes with your children, making it an exciting game! Pre-planned escape route will lessen confusion for all, including households with elderly or handicapped individuals.

A FAMILY MEETING PLACE

Decide on a nearby place to meet—maybe a neighbor's house—should your family need to evacuate the home due to fire (or any other emergency). Also, agree on a place outside the immediate area—local grocery store, for example—if you need to get some distance away, or if other family members are coming from different places when disaster strikes. A pre-determined place to meet will lessen anxiety.

DOCUMENT PERSONAL PROPERTY

In case property is destroyed, it helps to have documentation of ownership. The easiest way to document your property is to take photos or videos of the interior and exterior of your home and outbuildings. Be sure to include your personal belongings that may not be readily visible when you shoot your video or photos. Supporting documents of major purchases is also helpful.

CHECKLIST FOR FIRES IN THE HOME

I have an adequate number of battery-operated smoke detectors in good working order, placed strategically (bedrooms, kitchen, rooms with fireplace, etc.).   Yes   No

My smoke detectors also detect carbon monoxide.   Yes   No

I have made a floor plan of my home and marked two escape routes from each room.   Yes   No

I have posted the escape routes in each child's room at his or her eye level, and each child understands what to do.   Yes   No

I have a fire extinguisher of the ABC type.   Yes   No

I know how to use it.   Yes   No

My family members know how to use it.   Yes   No

I need an emergency escape ladder(s).   Yes   No

I have purchased the escape ladder(s) needed.   Yes   No

I have chosen a place near my home and also outside of the immediate area for my family to meet.   Yes   No

I have taken photos or videoed my home, in and out.   Yes   No

FAMILY COMMUNICATIONS

Planning how to contact family members in the event of an emergency or disaster will greatly relieve concerns for everyone. Complete a contact card for every family member. Have each person carry a personal copy.

For families with children, consider sending this information to the schools for their records. Schools keep emergency contact information on all children, of course, but I am suggesting a more detailed contact list.

MEDICAL RELEASE FORMS

Fill out a medical release form for each child's school to keep on file in case of an emergency when you cannot be reached.

FAMILY CONTACT INFORMATION

For each family member, include in your Disaster Preparedness Plan Notebook (see Chapter 11) pictures that will clearly show features (such as passport photos) in case it is necessary to notify authorities should family members become separated.

If you have family members living outside of your area or state, share this contact information with them and develop a plan of notification to let them know your status. Friends and other relatives can all be part of the notification network.

Information to fill out for each family member:

Contact name: _____

Telephone (Home): _____

Telephone (Cell): _____

E-mail address : _____

Out-of-state contact name: _____

Telephone (Home): _____

Telephone (Cell): _____

E-mail address: _____

Neighborhood meeting place:_____

Meeting place telephone :_____

Dial 911 in emergencies (Place this number on each card.)

Additional important phone numbers and information:

_____

_____

_____

It is easy to share this information in non-emergency situations **(this means do it now!)**, particularly electronically, but be sure to make hard copies and place a copy in waterproof containers as part of your emergency kits! (See Appendix J.)

In the event of a major national catastrophe that disrupts all normal communication and evacuation of an area is necessary, consider planning with your entire family a safe place to gather—such as the home of a family member who lives in an area not affected by the catastrophe. Make back-up plans.

PREPAID PHONE CARDS

Each family member, including the smaller, school-age children, should carry a prepaid phone card at all times.

UTILITY SHUT-OFF AND SAFETY

Following a disaster, it may become necessary to shut off utility services at your home.

Downed power lines or the risk of sparks igniting natural gas may necessitate shutting down all electricity to your home. You must know where the circuit box is located and how to shut it off.

For your safety, shut off all individual electrical circuits before shutting off the main circuit breaker!

Natural gas leaks and risk for explosions and fires is a significant risk following some disasters. It is vital to know how to shut off the natural gas to your home. Contact your local gas company to learn the proper procedure.

Never turn the gas back on by yourself once it has been turned off! Get a qualified professional to turn it back on!

Water is always a vital resource, never more so than following a disaster. Broken water lines may contaminate the water supply to your home. It is often wise to shut off the main water valve to your home until you have been notified that the water is safe to drink.

The effects of gravity may cause your hot water heater and toilet tanks to drain unless you turn off the water at the main valve to your home.

Locate the main water valve to your home and make sure everyone in your household knows where it is located. Label the valve with a tag for easy identification.

ELECTRICITY, GAS AND WATER
UTILITIES SHUT-OFF
Checklist

I know where my electricity circuit box is located.	Yes	No
I know how to shut off electricity to the entire house.	Yes	No
I have taught all responsible household members how to shut off electricity to the whole house.	Yes	No
I have contacted my local gas company and know how to properly shut off all gas appliances and gas service to my home.	Yes	No

I have taught all responsible household members how to properly shut off all gas appliances and gas services to my home.	Yes	No
I know where the main water valve to my home is located, and I know how to shut it off.	Yes	No
I have taught all responsible household members how to properly shut off the main water valve.	Yes	No

CARING FOR INDIVIDUALS WITH SPECIAL NEEDS

Many families have unique special needs with personal handicaps, handicapped family members, or elderly family members who need special attention and preparation for their care during emergencies. Other family members may have diseases or disorders that require individualized planning.

In addition, some of you may have neighbors or other community members who need individualized care and may require your assistance. I address individual and neighborhood preparedness in the next chapter.

BETTER A NEIGHBOR NEARBY

"Do not wait for leaders; do it alone, person to person."

—Mother Teresa

"[Residents'] involvement needs to be applicable to their day-to-day life. If it is about their children, they will come. About community improvement, maybe. If the purpose is far-reaching, no."

—Resident
Providence, Rhode Island

"And do not go to your brother's house when disaster strikes you — better a neighbor nearby than a brother far away."

—Proverbs 27:10

CHAPTER 5

WHEN ALL PLANS FAIL
INDIVIDUAL AND NEIGHBORHOOD PREPAREDNESS

"Do not wait for leaders; do it alone, person to person." Mother Teresa was a woman of wisdom and resourcefulness. She practiced what she preached in the dirty streets of Calcutta, where she saw Jesus in the face of every beggar she met. She didn't wait for the government to launch a program. She didn't wait for relief workers. She was a committee of one, empowered by the Holy Spirit, to impact her culture. For her, ministry was a matter of individual responsibility, "individual preparedness."

INDIVIDUAL PREPAREDNESS

Too many people in the United States have gotten used to the idea that it is the responsibility of the government—whether local, state, or national— to take care of emergencies or respond to disasters. For most disasters and emergencies, this works out just fine. But as Katrina so vividly demonstrated, when hundreds of thousands of people are affected at one time, the normal emergency structures are overwhelmed and the state of individual preparedness becomes crucial.

Even in more minor emergencies, it will sometimes take days for relief teams to assist all those who need help. Obviously, the more people who are prepared, the less strain on available emergency resources.

I have already touched on the importance of physical fitness and nutrition in Chapter 3 and also listed the important items to include in emergency kits at home, in the car, and at work. But even as I write this, I am thinking of the thousands of people who do not have personal automobiles or use them infrequently and have to rely on public transportation. If this applies to you, the wisdom of carrying some emergency kit items with you at all times becomes a major consideration. Since emergencies are often unexpected, some experts recommend such a personal kit for everyone.

Just remember that airports and many public buildings will not allow all the recommended emergency supply items to be brought into the building. Check it out before putting an item in your personal kit. For instance, I had a small multi-tool device taken from me at an airport several years ago, before I knew the rules!

Below, I list what a bare-bones emergency kit should contain if one decides to carry it at all times, either in a belt-pouch, purse, or briefcase. I have excluded items that would be prohibited at airports or federal public buildings.

BARE-BONES PERSONAL EMERGENCY KIT

Flashlight, small, waterproof   _____

Whistle   _____

First aid kit, small   _____

Water purification tablets   _____

Smoke hood or partial face respirator,   _____
particularly advisable if you live in
a high-rise, or ride on subways.
(See Appendix H for options.)

Cord (550-lb. test, monofilament fishing line   _____
(minimum 30 feet)

ADDITIONAL BASIC PERSONAL
EMERGENCY KIT ITEMS

If airports and restricted public buildings are not an issue, the following basic personal emergency kit items are recommended in addition to those listed above:

Multi-tool (e.g., Leatherman or Kershaw   _____
locking pliers)

Mini-pry bar   _____

Weatherproof matches   _____

EMT shears (bandage scissors)   _____

Energy bars   _____

Money   _____

Another very practical recommendation is to wear good walking shoes when traveling, or at least have a good pair of shoes handy should the need arise to run or quickly evacuate an area. Boots made of Gore-Tex would be the best to meet most any type of emergency.

Attempting to write recommendations for individuals who live in high-rise apartments in densely populated cities as well as those who live in a rural setting is something of a challenge. In this chapter, I am identifying and addressing in more depth some of the unique individual preparedness steps that some people will need to take and also relate these preparations to neighborhood planning.

NEIGHBORHOOD PREPAREDNESS

Do you live in downtown New York City or in rural Oklahoma? The term *neighborhood* conjures up totally different images in your mind, depending upon where you live.

Some type of neighborhood planning will be helpful for everyone, however, no matter what your living situation. For many, this will be a greater problem than for others, but to whatever extent possible—even if it is only one neighbor you can trust—any neighborhood planning will be to your advantage.

This kind of planning is distinct from networking your church or community. There will be times when a close neighbor will be the only immediate source of assistance, no matter how good your local emergency teams or how well developed your church network strategy. (See Chapter 8.

As Proverbs 27:10 reminds us: *"Do not go to your brother's house when disaster strikes you—better a neighbor nearby than a brother far away."*

GETTING TO KNOW YOUR NEIGHBORS

If you have good relations with your neighbors or are part of a homeowners' association, it will be relatively easy to get together with others in your neighborhood and plan your response to anticipated emergencies. The sad truth, though, is that neighbors often do not know each other well, if at all. Busyness, two-income families, single-parent families, poverty, violence in the inner cities, and other factors have left us fragmented as a society.

Most of you who are reading this book are followers of Jesus. The situation described above presents both a challenge and an opportunity to get to know your neighbors and hopefully, somewhere along the line, share your faith with unbelievers. Calling a meeting for the purpose of emergency preparedness will often be a true "door-opener."

Remember the quote at the beginning of this chapter made by a resident in a poor community in Providence, Rhode Island? "[Residents'] involvement needs to be applicable to their day-to-day life. If it is about their children, they will come. About community improvement, maybe. If the purpose is far-reaching, no."

Neighborhood emergency planning is definitely applicable to each resident and meets all the criteria of the statement above.

Obviously, no blanket advice can be given for all situations. In instances where it would not be wise to initiate these neighborhood get-togethers by yourself, go with those you trust to meet other neighbors and see if they would be interested in joining your planning group. You can surely find at least one neighbor who will cooperate and plan with you.

TWO ARE BETTER THAN ONE

Two are better than one, because they have a good return for their work: If one falls down, his friend can help him up. But pity the man who falls and has no one to help him up!

Also, if two lie down together, they will keep warm. But how can one keep warm alone? Though one may be overpowered, two can defend themselves. A cord of three strands is not quickly broken.

—Ecclesiastes 4:9-12

Notice how many aspects of help are afforded by having at least two people working together. More work gets done. One helps the other up if injury occurs. The problems of cold and self-defense are addressed and resolved, and if you can get a third neighbor involved, the benefits are exponential.

EMERGENCY COMMUNICATION

During the aftermath of Hurricane Katrina, communication became a nightmare. Phone communications were down and even if available, the circuits were overloaded. Even satellite phones did not work well in many instances.

Remember these tips if an emergency arises in which all lines of communication are down:

PHONE TIPS

Tip 1: It is important to have at least one corded phone in the home. Corded phones will often work even when the electrical power to the home is off since they are powered through the phone lines.

Tip 2: Pay phones may work even when home phones do not.

Tip 3: If you need to charge your cell phones, do not forget the car charger.

Tip 4: Hand-crank and solar chargers for cell phones are also available.

Communication with your family and neighbors will be of vital importance. Know your neighbors' phone numbers, both land line and cellular. Also get E-mail addresses just in case Internet communication is still available.

NEIGHBORS' INFORMATION CHECKLIST

I have my neighbors' landline phone numbers.	Yes	No
I have my neighbors' cell phone numbers.	Yes	No
I have my neighbors' E-mail addresses.	Yes	No
I have shared my information with neighbors.	Yes	No

FREE HIGH-SPEED INTERNET COMMUNICATION

Several high-speed Internet communication companies are currently available: VoIP, Voice over Internet Protocol, such as Vonage. However, I want to alert you to a VoIP carrier, Skype. When both parties use Skype, it is free; otherwise, there is a charge. One can conference in up to nine people at one time. The system works internationally as well. I use Skype frequently to keep in touch with my family when I am overseas as well as in the U.S.

TWO-WAY RADIO TRANSMITTERS

You should prepare for the times when all the normal means of communication are not available during a disaster. At such times two-way radio transmitters would be the best way to communicate for most people. This works well for family members as well as neighbors.

The more powerful transmitters are the General Mobile Radio Service radios (GMRS). These radios have a 5-25 mile operating range. The only drawback to these units is that a Federal Communications Commission license is needed to operate them.

Walkie-talkies (Family Radio Service band) are less expensive and do not require an FCC license. However, they provide a much shorter distance of communication, from a half-mile up to five miles in open areas. Our grandchildren have great fun with some of these walkie-talkies, but one must be sure to keep plenty of batteries and/or have the ability to recharge batteries.

Having some type of communication is comforting to all parties involved and at times will be life-saving. Having a family and neighborhood communication system in place could prove vital.

NOAA WEATHER RADIO

I have already suggested that you consider purchasing a National Oceanic & Atmospheric Administration weather radio receiver for your family if you live in an area where adverse weather is annually one of your "horse" emergencies. It would be a great idea for your neighborhood group to have at least one. You could keep each other informed of emergency weather bulletins via your two-way radio transmitters if the other means of communication are down.

RADIO SCANNERS

A radio scanner that scans emergency frequencies used by the police, military and other emergency responders is another item that you might want to purchase for yourself and/or for the neighborhood group. The information transmitted over these frequencies may prove very helpful in times of disaster or major crisis. Many truckers use Citizen Band (CB) sets to communicate traffic information with each other.

HAM RADIOS

Are you or is anyone in your neighborhood a HAM radio operator? This person must be licensed. HAM radios can provide local and even international communication via shortwave broadcasts during emergencies. HAM operators frequently coordinate government and non-government relief agencies (NGOs).

Having served in medical mission work for 25 years, I can attest to the effectiveness of this vital link that at times has been the only link missionaries have had during certain emergencies.

PRE-DISASTER PLANNING

The more detailed you make your personal and neighborhood emergency plans before any disaster strikes, the greater will be the benefit for everyone. There may be times when evacuation is needed and it is very conceivable that neighbors helping each other may make a great difference in the safety of all.

In Chapter 7, I address preparations for the elderly and handicapped which will be a necessary part of any neighborhood planning.

BE GOOD NEIGHBORS

I love the quote attributed to Mother Teresa: "I can do things you cannot do. You can do things I cannot do. Together we can do great things."

As in the examples of sharing NOAA radios, two-way transmitters, and radio scanner information among all parties, there will often be certain aspects of disaster preparedness in which one neighbor may have greater skills than the others and be able to share his or her expertise. Your neighbors might include doctors, nurses, EMTs (emergency medical technicians) or other individuals with first-aid and first-responder experience.

For instance, when our electric power was lost following an ice storm, we were left without heat for more than four days. Our closest neighbor uses only a wood-burning heater during the winter and was not affected by the ice storm. Since I was out of town, our neighbors took care of my wife and kept her warm in my absence. As a result of that experience, I'm planning to install a wood-burning stove in our home!

On our part, we have a 30,000-gallon swimming pool that can be used as a water source in emergencies for such things as bathing or flushing toilets. With water filtration and purification systems, it can also be used for drinking. This is a resource available to my small neighborhood.

Let me give a hypothetical situation where the risk of flooding is a real potential emergency. Suppose one of your neighbors has a boat that can accommodate only six people. If evacuation over water becomes necessary, it should be pre-planned how this would be done. If the needs of the neighborhood could not be met with available resources, a decision would have to be made as to the need for provision of inflatable rafts or other boats to be used by the neighbors. Either each family could supply their own solution, or the group could collectively purchase whatever was deemed necessary to meet any flooding threat.

Living in a rural area as we do has its benefits. Some of our neighbors have goats, which can provide milk and other milk products. Other neighbors have chickens. I know, of course, that most Americans do not live in rural areas, so we will be focusing more on the challenges faced by urban and suburban America.

SPECIAL EMERGENCY SITUATIONS

Several unique emergency situations are not covered in most of the disaster preparedness books. Prayerfully consider situations that you are facing that will require special preparations. If you happen to be one of these people, then be sure to inform your family and neighbors as appropriate.

ESCAPING FROM A SUBWAY

Tens of thousands of people in the United States commute via subway every day. If you are one of them, it would be wise to heed these recommendations. I am approaching this subject from the standpoint of natural and accidental hazards. For an informative animated instruction guide to evacuating a subway in an emergency, go to *http://wmata.com/ riding/safety/evac.swf.* This is an excellent guide provided especially for persons living in or visiting the D. C. area.

If you regularly ride on a subway, carry a flashlight. Be sure it is a non-incendive type that will not create any sparks that could set off an explosion if certain gases were present. Also, carry a mini-pry bar. In addition, you should have with you a smoke escape hood, which should provide you with 15-20 minutes of breathable air in the event of a fire. Each of these items is already in your personal emergency kit if you followed the earlier recommendations.

If you do not have an escape hood, cover your nose and mouth with your coat, shirt, blouse or tie. If water is available, wet the clothing before pressing against your face. This should buy you one or two minutes of extra time to escape.

Normally the safest place during a subway emergency is inside the subway train car. You should leave the train car only if you are threatened by fire.

If evacuation from the train car is needed, this is a good time to have followed the suggestion to wear good shoes! If possible, stay close to the subway conductor or to the other evacuees ahead of you and take the first emergency exit.

Learn how to recognize the "third rail" of the subway tracks, which is the electric power source for the subway. *KEEP AWAY FROM THE **THIRD** RAIL AT ALL TIMES!*

EVACUATION FROM A HIGH-RISE BUILDING

If you live in a high-rise building, this is, in fact, your neighborhood. Fires in a high-rise, whether in an office setting, hotel, apartment, or condominium, are extremely dangerous. It is often difficult for emergency rescue teams to reach higher floors or to get to the side or back of the building.

Fire codes require that newer high-rise buildings be designed to contain fires to localized areas. Also, water sprinkler systems are usually required. Many buildings are "grandfathered" in, however, and do not meet newer fire safety standards.

If you live or work in a high-rise building, you need to establish your own disaster preparedness plan and escape routes. The following is a checklist of things to have, to know, or to prepare for.

CHECKLIST FOR EVACUATING A HIGH-RISE

I know the locations of every exit in my building.	Yes	No
I have checked the exits to be sure none are locked and that the exits are not blocked.	Yes	No
I have planned my escape route(s) in case of fire.	Yes	No
My building conducts fire drills. (If not, ask management to do so.)	Yes	No
I have reported any fire hazards to the local fire department. (Follow up on this.)	Yes	No
I have a flashlight (high-powered, non-incendive).	Yes	No
I have smoke escape hoods for family members and/or at work for myself.	Yes	No
All of my family know how to use the hoods.	Yes	No
I have determined it is feasible and advisable to have an escape ladder in my living quarters and I have obtained it.	Yes	No
I have determined it is feasible and advisable to have an escape ladder in my workplace and I have obtained it (or my employer has).	Yes	No
My building has an emergency light system. (If not, insist on getting one installed.)	Yes	No
My building elevators have pry bars to open jammed doors.	Yes	No
At the exits of my building, the following emergency items are mounted: pry bar, axe and a claw tool.	Yes	No
An ABC fire extinguisher is located at every	Yes	No

exit and entrance of my building.

In addition to the above recommendations, you may want to consider obtaining fire blankets for your home and/or office. Perhaps your employer would consider purchasing them for the employees.

PASSING YOUR KNOWLEDGE ON

In a very real sense, if you have now gained the knowledge about what to do in case of a subway incident or a high-rise fire, don't just keep the information to yourself. Yes, act on the information and prepare yourself and your family for such emergencies, but also take some responsibility to share this knowledge with your neighbors and co-workers.

SPIRITUAL PREPARATION FOR DISASTERS

Just as physical fitness and good nutrition are foundational to disaster preparedness, so is spiritual preparedness.

During the time I was writing this book, the I-35 westbound bridge into Minneapolis, Minnesota, collapsed with the tragic loss of lives. There could have been many more.

I was forwarded an E-mail with the testimony of a Christian young man who was within 100 feet of the bridge just before it collapsed. He said he had experienced a vision of the event before it happened. He felt as if the Holy Spirit was telling him to "stop!" He obeyed.

Irate drivers behind him honked their horns. Some tried to drive around his car at first, until the bridge suddenly gave way before their eyes! People came up to him afterward to thank him for stopping.

It is amazing to think that the lives of others may be so greatly affected by our sensitivity to hear from the Lord, especially during times of disaster. It is an awesome responsibility to remain spritually sensitive for the protection of ourselves, our family, and our neighbors.

FAIL-SAFE

"Should there be a loss of cabin pressure, an overhead compartment will automatically open and oxygen masks will fall down. Grab the mask closest to you and pull down on the plastic tubing. Put your own mask on first before trying to assist others who may need your help."

—Flight attendant giving instructions just before takeoff.

If anyone does not provide for his relatives, and especially for his immediate family, he has denied the faith and is worse than an unbeliever.
                                            —1 Timothy 5:8

In this same way, husbands ought to love their wives as their own bodies. He who loves his wife loves himself.

—Ephesians 5:28

CHAPTER 6

PUT YOUR OWN MASK ON FIRST
TAKING CARE OF YOUR FAMILY

As a father and grandfather, I found myself approaching this chapter with the "heart of a father" and a strong desire to protect my family. There is much more to protecting my family than just knowing what to put into a Grab-and-Go bag or how to respond to specific disasters.

What if something happens to me? How will my family get by without me? What if my home and personal records and documents are destroyed in a fire or tornado or other disaster? What if I lose my job? Is my "house in order"?

My wife, Sofia, and I have four children and six grandchildren. We are empty-nesters, yet I still want to be part of the planning for disaster preparedness for my extended family.

This chapter deals with the protection of family assets and family personal identity. One often hears today of identity theft, however, this is not what I am emphasizing in this chapter. I am concerned about the possibility of a significant disaster destroying not only your personal property, but also most, if not all, of your important documents. In this chapter you will learn how to prevent this "identity loss"!

My wife Sofia and her family actually suffered identity loss following the events of World War II. My wife's mother, Maria, then a teenager, had been taken from Ukraine as a prisoner of war and became part of the forced labor in Germany. My wife was born in a displaced persons' camp after the war. Her father, too, had been a prisoner of war and died after WWII ended.

Sofia, her sister, Nina, mother and stepfather, Josef, came to the U.S. via Ellis Island with minimal documentation. I remember their stories of what it meant to have almost no documentation of one's family and history. It took years to rebuild the family history. My wife had only one picture of her father which was the size of a passport photo. We are not even sure how to spell his name.

As I evaluated my feelings about these issues, I thought of the single-parent families that comprise almost 50 percent of family units in the United States. I also thought about the high divorce rate and broken homes and had the sense that I wanted this book to be practical and helpful for all families, no matter how the family unit is configured.

For those families with a mother and father present, preparation for disasters should be more readily doable, yet every family needs to prepare. This makes Chapter 8 particularly relevant to help meet the needs of some of the single-parent and special needs families.

If anyone does not provide for his relatives,
and especially for his immediate family,
he has denied the faith and is worse than an unbeliever.

−1 Timothy 5:8

I know it will not be easy for many to do all that is recommended in this book. To look at the "mountain" and do nothing, however, should not be your choice. I am reminded of the old Chinese proverb: "The longest journey begins with the first step!"

Hopefully, neighbors and church members will be able to come alongside and help if the task is emotionally overwhelming. Don't be afraid to ask for help.

PUTTING YOUR OWN MASK ON FIRST

Putting your mask on first is not a selfish act. Family members and possibly neighbors may be dependent on you. This is particularly true if you have small children, elderly parents in the home, or handicapped family members. These specialized situations will be addressed in Chapter 7.

I want to re-emphasize the need to become as physically fit as possible. Your ability to respond to disasters and to be a help and not a liability during emergencies is greatly impacted by your state of fitness and health.

If you have an illness that is beyond your ability to manage, I can understand. Most people who are not physically fit, however, need to choose to become more fit. This applies to spiritual fitness as well!

GETTING YOUR HOUSE IN ORDER

If you are responsible for planning for the welfare of your family, several major areas need to be addressed—and the sooner the better! Financial plans, credit card debt, your will or trusts, insurances on your home or properties, auto, health and life are just some of those areas.

FINANCIAL QUESTIONS TO ANSWER

- Do you have major debt?

- Do you have credit card debt?

- Do you pay high interest rates on credit cards?

- Do you have a plan to pay off credit cards within a relatively short time?

- Do you barely get by from paycheck to paycheck?

- Do you have a savings account that you contribute to on a monthly basis?

- Are you living within your means or is your indebtedness increasing each month, each year?

- Do you buy impulsively?

- Do you have a budget? Do you follow it?

- Who in your family has the better financial management skills?

- Do you pay your bills on time?

- Do you tithe?

- Do you give to charities?

And the list of questions could go on and on!

If your financial "house" is not in order, get help. Good debt-counseling and general financial services are available. One of the best Christian resources is Crown Financial Ministries that offers a wide range of financial tools and even free consultation services. For information, go to *www.crown.org*. A free volunteer financial counselor may be located near you. I also recommend books by Dave Ramsey, including *The Total Money Makeover.* For more information, go to *www.daveramsey.com.*

Managing your finances well and relieving the stress of financial pressures will go a long way toward helping you become better prepared for emergencies and potential disasters.

Some people recommend Suze Orman who offers advice on debt cancellation, wills, trusts, insurances needed, retirement, and investments. For more information, go to *www.suzeorman.com.*

TIPS ON BANK AND SAVINGS ACCOUNTS

I do not consider myself a financial counselor in any way. I have, however, come across some basic tips I want to share with you regarding bank and savings accounts.

Many people have not even taken the time to open a savings or money market account. Do it! Even if you are trying to pay off debts rapidly, be sure to institute a savings program for unexpected emergencies.

Tip #1: Shop for a bank that offers you free monthly checking, free checks, and free check writing. Go to *www.bankrate.com* to shop for no-fee checking accounts.

Tip #2: Make sure your bank and savings accounts are insured by the FDIC.

Tip #3: If you are comfortable doing your banking online, consider using a bank that provides online access to your statements and has a free online bill-paying service.

Tip #4: Make sure that there are no fees for ATM withdrawals.

Tip #5: Monitor your bank balances closely. Overdraft fees are incredibly costly. Online service makes this easy. Keep your check register in your checkbook up to date and accurate. Balance your checkbook monthly.

Tip #6: Have your paycheck automatically deposited into your checking account, and also authorize your bank to automatically transfer money each month into your savings or money market account. This will help you build up an emergency fund.

Tip #7: Set your savings account/money market account goal to cover six to eight months of living expenses.

Tip #8: Check out Internet banks that offer higher annual percentage yields (APYs). For further information, go to:

- Emigrant-Direct: *www.emigrant-direct.com*
- HSBC: *www.hsbcdirect.com*
- ING Direct: *www.ingdirect.com*

CREDIT CARDS

It is unconscionable how credit card companies and banks entice people to go into debt with "easy money." Even worse is the fact that those who can afford it least get socked with the highest interest rates that meet the biblical definition of usury. The whole system is wrong! Credit cards make it too easy to respond to impulse buying.

Credit card debt is just plain bad debt. If you do not pay off your credit card balances in full each month, you need to:

- Cut up your credit cards.
- Get financial counseling.
- Make a plan to pay off all credit card debt.
- Seek a good debt-counseling service.
- *Never* use home equity to pay off credit card debt.

If something should happen to you, any savings and assets you own will be sought by the credit card companies, and they will be paid first—even before your children!

INSURANCES

Sufficient insurance coverage for your life and property is extremely important, if you can at all afford them. Even as I write these words, I am acutely aware that many reading this book may not be able to follow through on all the recommendations. I will, however, list those I believe to be most helpful. If you cannot take all the suggested steps now, you will at least have an outline of goals to aim for.

Life Insurance: Do you need it? The answer is yes, if there is anyone in your life who is dependent on your income to live (such as your spouse or children and possibly your parents if they depend on you for their care.) If your current assets upon your death would cover these anticipated expenses, then the answer would be no.

The question is often asked, "How long should I have life insurance?" The answer is until you have accumulated sufficient assets to support your surviving spouse and/or children.

I do not want to advise you as to how much life insurance you should have. I would urge you to consider **only** guaranteed renewable term life insurance and **never** whole life insurance. Buy a policy from a life insurance company with a rating of "A" or better.

If your employer provides life insurance, that is good. If you need more insurance than your employer provides, however, it is usually more cost effective to purchase additional life insurance on your own, particularly if you are in good health.

Single Parents with Small Children As Beneficiaries: I have come across financial advice that will be of particular importance to single parents. A number of financial advisors recommend that single parents set up a revocable living trust as the best way to solve the dilemma of having small children as beneficiaries of your life insurance policy or your estate.

Here is the problem. Life insurance companies will not make payouts to children under the age of 18 or to their guardians. This is true even if you have stated in your will who the guardian of your children will be. The life insurance company will require a state-appointed guardian, which may cost thousands of dollars. A court order will normally be required each time funds are accessed by the guardian. This could get expensive!

On the other hand, if a revocable trust has not been set up, your life insurance funds and estate could be given in their entirety to your child at the age of eighteen. Not a good idea!

If you have designated a revocable living trust as the beneficiary of your estate and life insurance, the successor trustee that you have designated will manage the funds and assets for your child(ren).

Home Insurance: If you have a home mortgage, chances are you have been required by your mortgage company to carry home insurance. This does not mean that you have adequate coverage!

Take the time to make sure that you will be fully compensated if your home is damaged or destroyed. Make sure you know what hazards are covered and which are not. Many Katrina victims had to deal with home insurance policies that did not cover them adequately, yet they were still liable for the mortgage even when the home was destroyed!

HOME INSURANCE QUESTIONS TO ANSWER

1. How much will your policy pay you if your home is totally destroyed?

_____

2. Does your policy coverage increase annually to   Yes   No
keep up with inflation?

3. What living expenses will your policy cover if you cannot live in your home during any required rebuilding or repairs?

_____

4. Are the personal possessions in your home   Yes   No
adequately covered?

5. What are your personal liability coverage limits in case you are sued (e.g., someone falls and is injured on your property)?

_____

6. Do you need flood insurance? (Standard policies   Yes   No
   do not cover this; discuss with insurance agent; go
to *www.floodsmart.gov/floodsmart/pages/index.jsp* to
determine flood risk for homes or businesses in the
U.S. They can also help you find a flood insurance agent).

7. Do you need earthquake insurance? (Standard   Yes   No
policies do not cover this; discuss with insurance
agent.)

8. Do you need hurricane coverage? (Standard   Yes   No
policies do not cover this; discuss with insurance
agent.)

9. What type of dwelling limit coverage do you have?

Guaranteed replacement cost coverage (Best)	Yes	No
or		
Extended replacement cost coverage (Good)	Yes	No
or		
Replacement cost coverage (Puts you at some risk to pay out-of-pocket replacement costs.)	Yes	No
or		
Actual cash-value coverage (Unacceptable. Poor insurance only covers depreciated repair values.)	Yes	No

10. I have documented my personal possessions   Yes   No
in my home for insurance claim purposes.

11. If you rent, do you have adequate renter's   Yes   No
insurance to cover the value of your possessions
and any personal liability?

12. Do your assets exceed $500,000?   Yes   No
(Consider buying a personal umbrella policy.)

Health Insurance: Healthcare costs have skyrocketed over the past several decades. It bothers me a great deal that so many do not have adequate health insurance and many do not have any health insurance at all. Get health insurance if you can afford it. If it means selling the car you love and settling for a less expensive model, do it.

Accidents remain the number-one killer and cause of disability in the U.S.A. We also face the threat of biological terrorism; however, this is a "zebra." Accidents and common illnesses are the "horses" and need to be anticipated and prepared for, if at all possible.

If several health insurance options are offered through your employer, opt for the one with the best coverage, not just the one with the least out-of-pocket, up-front costs. Healthcare expenses can take a huge chunk out of your paycheck and also deplete savings very quickly should you need emergency care or hospitalization.

If you are married and both are working, take the best health coverage offered between you and make sure your children are covered, even if you have to pay out of pocket for the extra coverage.

Disability Insurance: I mention this insurance to be thorough in my

TAKING CARE OF YOUR FAMILY

recommendations, though I know many will not be able to consider this. The statistical chance of being disabled from an accident or injury is far greater than premature death. If your employer offers this benefit, great.

If you have to choose, health and life insurance policies would take priority over disability insurance.

Automobile Insurance: It is illegal to drive a vehicle without insurance. It is also foolish. Liability insurance is mandatory. Whether or not you get comprehensive insurance to cover theft, hail damage, etc., is your call, depending on the value of your car. My only admonition is not to be "penny-wise and pound-foolish" by failing to take out adequate coverage just to reduce the premiums.

When I first obtained auto insurance years ago, I did not realize that the term "collision" premium only covered my vehicle. The "liability" portion of the insurance covers any payments for damage to the other car or passengers.

If you are making payments on your vehicle, your lender required you to take out full insurance, has a lien against your car, and will receive any insurance payments first if the car is "totaled." At least you will not be stuck with car payments and no car!

WILLS AND TRUSTS

Again, I have to put in a disclaimer that I am not a financial advisor! Many financial advisors agree that you should have three essential documents:

1. **A will; this is a must, but not sufficient by itself.**

2. **A revocable living trust with an incapacity clause.**

3. **An advance directive and durable power of attorney for health care.**

Consult your attorney if you do not already have these important documents in place. Legal fees could run from several hundred to several thousand dollars. Inexpensive do-it-yourself kits to create will and trust documents are available, but make sure they meet state and federal requirements!

IMPORTANT DOCUMENTS AND STORAGE

This topic has been covered to some extent in Chapter 4. For a more complete list of items requiring special handling, refer to Appendix E. The crucial thing is to determine what needs to go with you in your Grab-and-Go bag and what needs to be stored in such places as a safe deposit box.

DIGITAL SURVIVAL

Are many of your critical family records and documents on your computer? Do you operate a small business out of your home?

I cannot express to you how critical it is to back up your entire hard drives on a frequent basis. I learned this the hard way when my computer hard drive just stopped working one day. I had backed up my critical financial data, but unfortunately lost some of my digital pictures of my family and grandchildren that I could not replace!

Not only should you make backup copies of your files, you should store copies of critical information in an off-site location, preferably over fifty miles away from your home to decrease the chance of your storage area being destroyed along with your home or office.

One little trick I have learned, when I do not have a flash storage drive with me, is to E-mail important documents as attachments to my Internet E-mail server. This gets stored on my Internet server, which I can access from any computer at any time. I actually was able to retrieve several important documents that way when my hard drive suddenly crashed. The better way, of course, is to have a disk or flash drive backup.

Don't forget to unplug your expensive electrical equipment and computers during electrical storms. Surge protectors are a must, not only for your equipment, but also for your phone lines. Another expensive lesson I learned occurred when my fax line, which was hooked up to my all-purpose copier, "blew" and rendered the copier inoperative.

Those of you with small businesses operating out of your home may want to invest in a power backup unit (uninterruptible power supply—UPS) and not just surge protectors. These units will give you time to copy any unsaved critical data before you shut down your computer.

DOCUMENTS TO KEEP ON YOUR PERSON
AT ALL TIMES

If evacuation of your home is necessary, there are certain documents that you should keep on your person at all times, with copies in waterproof containers in your Grab-and-Go bag.

I do a lot of international traveling and have a travel pouch that fits around my waist and under my clothing. I put critical documents, such as my passport, in that pouch. In some emergencies, I may become separated from my Grab-and-Go bag, but it is much less likely that I'll be separated from the pouch around my waist. There are times I have slept with the pouch on in situations when I did not feel it was safe to remove it. Following this principle, I have never lost my passport nor had it stolen in all my travels to 105 countries.

Remember, I am recommending a pouch that is hidden under your clothing, not worn on the outside. There are many different styles of pouches that can be worn under clothing. The one I use is long and thin, and stored items can be spread out to decrease bulk. Most people cannot tell I am wearing a waist pouch.

Have each older family member carry his or her own pouch. The adult who accompanies smaller children or handicapped individuals should carry the documents.

LIST OF POUCH DOCUMENTS
AND OTHER ITEMS

Passport _____

Driver's license _____

Social Security card(s) for self, family _____

Bank cards and/or credit cards _____

Money (most in the pouch, some in your pocket) _____

List of immunizations, with dates _____

Medical alert information (or wear tag or
        wristband) _____

List of critical family contact numbers _____

List of emergency numbers (police, fire, _____

hospitals, doctor, etc.)

Extra set of car and house keys   _____

Prepaid phone cards (See Appendix I.)   _____

FAMILY COMMUNICATION PLANS

In times of disaster, working out the details of how you will communicate with family members living with you as well as those living elsewhere, is vitally important. See Chapter 4 and Appendix J.

POSSIBLE TRAVEL CONSIDERATIONS

I have discussed the possibility of your having to evacuate your home by car or on foot, but have not brought up the possibility of travel by air. Some experts in disaster planning for families advise keeping enough cash reserves to cover the cost of flying your family to a safe haven.

THE TRUE SAFE HAVEN

Taking precautions and planning is prudent, but our true safety is in the Lord. You and I need to commit ourselves and our families into His care.

If you make the Most High your dwelling
   even the Lord, who is my refuge
then no harm will befall you,
   no disaster will come near your tent.
For he will command his angels concerning you
   to guard you in all your ways.

—Psalm 91:9-11

"BRIDGE OVER TROUBLED WATERS"

I have always enjoyed listening to the song, "Bridge Over Troubled Waters," by Simon and Garfunkel. In the context of this chapter—people with special needs in time of trouble—I think of being a bridge over "troubled waters," helping them to cross over safely.

CHAPTER 7

BRIDGE OVER TROUBLED WATER
PEOPLE WITH SPECIAL NEEDS

As a physician, I have been on a number of ambulance runs. Careful planning has gone into the design and equipping of those ambulances. An attempt is made to stock the ambulance with all the equipment and supplies needed to respond to almost any emergency. Hospitals must have a completely separate backup source of power should the normal utility service be interrupted.

This same careful planning is needed to care for the elderly, the handicapped, and small children during times of crisis. Careful planning also needs to be in place for those with special medical conditions, illnesses, or nutritional requirements. In addition, special assistance may be needed by non-English speaking persons. Community groups of the same cultural background may be able to help keep these people informed.

Another group of people that fits the category of "special needs" during times of disasters are those without personal transportation. Neighborhoods, communities, and church groups may all have to get involved in addition to local governments to help with this potentially huge logistic challenge. The Katrina disaster highlighted this problem. If you or your family members are part of this "no personal vehicle" group, make sure you pre-plan well.

Information about first aid kits and injury management is also included in this chapter because people, who were well and healthy before a disaster, may become injured or sick and be among the "handicapped" needing special care.

CARE CHALLENGES FOR THOSE WITH SPECIAL NEEDS

Having lost both of my parents within the past few years, I am keenly aware of the challenges faced by families caring for elderly members. My father passed away in 2006 after living several years with my sister. The final few months required someone to be available for his care 24/7.

During the last year of his life, my sister did have to deal with a hurricane going through Lakeland, Florida, but no evacuation was required, for which my family was grateful. I can only imagine the effort that would have been required to evacuate him along with other family members.

Two other categories of individuals needing special assistance are the physically handicapped (including deaf and blind) and the mentally handicapped who still live at home. Many of the challenges of providing assistance to these family members and friends are similar and I will group the discussion around personal support needs, equipment needs, and special supplies and medications.

Many disaster preparedness books do not spend much time on the topic of people with special needs. One reason for this is probably the fact that special attention is already being given to the care of these individuals and a support structure and system has often already been established. Also, planning for mobilization of this support structure in times of disaster is logistically difficult, to say the least, and often has to be tailored to each individual situation.

If you are elderly or physically handicapped and are still the primary decision-maker for your care, be sure to address these disaster preparation issues with your family, neighbors, church community, healthcare givers, and first-responder providers such as your local fire and rescue units.

For common emergencies, local fire and rescue units have often already identified the special needs individuals in their area of responsibility. In times of major disaster, these sources of help may well be overwhelmed, and individuals may need to rely on their own resources and help from their neighbors.

It goes without saying that the family's Grab-and-Go bag will have been planned with the routine and special-need items specifically required for elderly and handicapped family members.

ELDERLY AND HANDICAPPED LIVING ALONE

If you or family members are elderly or handicapped and living alone, plans for dealing with emergencies must be carefully worked out.

As a physician, I have observed many situations where elderly individuals live alone longer than they should. It is often difficult for the elderly to give up their independence or move from the family home. Many times children are reluctant to intervene. I know. I have "been there and bought the T-shirt"!

There may be no family to turn to. More and more often the nuclear family does not live close to each other. This unfortunate situation is made worse by the fact that many social services are being cut back due to decreased funding by the government and insurance companies.

If family is close by, you may be making the assumption that plans for emergency situations have been made by the family. I want to alert you, however, to consider your elderly and handicapped neighbors and inquire if such plans have, in fact, been worked out. If not, you may become the facilitator for getting your neighbor the help he or she needs in planning for emergencies.

ELDERLY AND HANDICAPPED LIVING WITH FAMILY

Eldercare at home is on the rise in our nation. This creates unique challenges to families, particularly in times of emergencies. Also, with advances in medicine, many more handicapped individuals are able to live at home with their family, using very specialized equipment.

It is not uncommon to be in homes with wheelchairs, motorized carts, hospital beds, oxygen tanks, ventilators, nebulizers, bedside commodes, and other portable medical devices. Some people routinely receive intravenous feedings, gastric tubes, peritoneal infusions, home cancer treatments and the list goes on and on.

The care-giving requirements for some family members can be incredibly great, sometimes to the detriment of the health of the caregiver. In times of emergencies and disasters, this care-giving need is multiplied and made much more difficult.

CHOOSE CARE-GIVING LOCATION IN HOME CAREFULLY

Consider an approaching tornado or threat of flood or hurricane. How do you respond when caring for elderly or handicapped family member(s)? One way to prepare for such emergencies would be to place the individual where moving would not be required. Often this is not practical. When facing the need to move an individual, you will have to consider the following:

It will often require two people to assist the very elderly or physically handicapped individuals in moving them to a safe place within the home or building, or if evacuation is required, to an appropriate vehicle. This needs to be a very central part of pre-disaster planning. If there are not two people in the family who can do this, pre-arrange the help of neighbors.

TRANSPORTATION

If transportation for the elderly or handicapped is part of the current care, the mechanics and logistics of getting out of the home and having an appropriate vehicle available may already be worked out. If reliance has been on a specialized service that provides care for many special needs individuals, however, it may not be available when a major disaster looms ahead or has already occurred.

A back-up transportation plan must be in place, not just a general back-up plan. Vehicles and specific people responsible need to be designated. There may not be an ideal vehicle available to handle all the equipment for an elderly or handicapped individual. Plan well in advance so that there is no last-minute confusion that may jeopardize the lives of everyone involved.

Do a "test run." One of your teenagers or friends could play the role of the handicapped or elderly for the test, if needed. If at all possible, it is best to utilize only one vehicle. Two vehicles may be required.

It is critical to have portable medical equipment such as portable oxygen or battery-powered nebulizers, if that is a requirement. You cannot be scrambling for this equipment at the last minute.

EVACUATION ROUTE FOR THOSE WITH SPECIAL NEEDS

If evacuation becomes necessary, be sure to plan a route that avoids staircases, hills, or rough terrain if any portion must be covered by foot. If this is impossible, the need for early evacuation for even potential disasters becomes paramount.

FLOOD EMERGENCIES

Families with special-need members should evacuate their homes well in advance of any rising water in the event of potential flooding. Trying to evacuate when the emergency is upon you will be so much more difficult. If unpredictable flooding is a significant risk, it is highly recommended that you obtain an inflatable raft or sport boat if you do not have one. This could become a neighborhood project.

I vividly remember seeing the rescue efforts of flood victims following Katrina. The risk of flooding in this area had been known for years and adequate individual and neighborhood preparations were not made. There were just not enough rescue boats available to reach all the people in time.

If you are considering purchasing a raft or small boat, there are battery-powered motors available if gasoline-powered motors and storage of gasoline are not practical. Cost and storage will obviously be significant factors in your decision.

HUNKERING DOWN

Depending on the emergency, there may be times that "hunkering down"—having one or two people remain with the elderly or handicapped person—is the only option while the rest of the family evacuates. Unfortunately, some elderly people have stubbornly refused to leave their family homes and suffered the consequences. Pray that you will never have to face this situation.

PRE-PACKAGE MEDICATIONS

Make sure medications needed for the special-needs family member(s) are pre-packaged and part of the Grab-and-Go bag. It is not uncommon for the elderly to be on many different medications, and it is also common to have medications change periodically. Be sure to update the list of meds on a regular basis. Update the list every time changes are made, and keep medications current in the Grab-and-Go bag. Keep at least one month's supply of medications taken regularly.

You may have to be creative in getting this extra stash of medication if you are on a limited budget and your insurance company won't cover these expenses. Perhaps your physician can help you with samples, or your social worker can "run interference" for you. There is usually a way to get around all the regulations. **Don't forget to exchange newly purchased medications and use the older prescriptions first.**

DIABETICS ON INSULIN

For individuals on insulin, planning will include a means of keeping insulin supplies at a cool temperature if refrigeration facilities are not available. If you or a neighbor has a camper with refrigeration on-board and you will be traveling together, this would be a great place for storage.

ALERTING DEAF INDIVIDUALS

If you or a family member is deaf, obtain a vibrating beeper if you do not already have one. This device can be used to alert the deaf individual to emergencies.

SANITATION AND HYGIENE

Sanitation and hygiene are very real problems for everyone during times of disaster, but particularly critical for caregivers of those who cannot toilet themselves. In addition to disposable diapers, have plenty of moist towelettes and hand sanitizers.

A urinal and bedpan may work better in some situations, not only for the handicapped and elderly, but also for the whole family. I remember being caught in a snowstorm in which the road exits were so deep in snow that the only safe option was to continue on the main highway without stopping. Needless to say, I had to improvise since I did not have a urinal in my car!

At times it would also not be safe to leave one's car. I think of the incredibly long lines of vehicles trying to leave New Orleans before Katrina hit. There was no place for normal sanitation. Plastic bottles and even Ziploc storage bags work well.

Chlorophyll tablets can greatly reduce fecal odor. This can help when caring for bed-ridden family members, either in the home or in a vehicle, when evacuation becomes necessary. You can also use kitty litter for solid waste and dispose of it in a plastic bag until you have time to bury it later.

CARING FOR INJURIES SUSTAINED IN A DISASTER

Remember to take the Red Cross training in first aid, if at all possible (*www.redcross.org)*, or training from a local healthcare provider. I also recommend a small pocketbook, *Disaster Survival Guide,* by Harris J. Andrews and Alexander Bowers. This book provides a quick reference to many basic emergency situations, including first aid.

A FEW BASIC FIRST AID GUIDELINES

1. Stop and look first! Don't immediately start helping an injured person without making sure it is safe to do so. For instance, if a person has possibly sustained a neck injury, it is imperative not to move the patient until proper immobilization of the neck has been accomplished. Another dangerous situation is electrocution. Do not touch a person who has been electrocuted until all electrical power has been turned off!

2. Call 911 immediately when you face an emergency beyond your ability and training to handle.

3. Do not move a victim, unless a life-threatening situation exists.

LEARN THE ABC'S OF FIRST AID

"A" is for airway. Make sure the victim's airway is not obstructed. This is the first thing to check for. I also use the "A" for alertness. Is the victim conscious, oriented, or disoriented? If you call 911 and speak to an emergency person, they will first ask, "Is the patient conscious?"

"B" is for breathing. Make sure the victim's airway is clear and he or she is breathing. If the person is not breathing, it may be necessary to apply mouth-to-mouth resuscitation. Recently new CPR guidelines have been published. Contact your local American Red Cross for more information.

"C" is for circulation. Is the victim in shock or bleeding excessively? Does the victim have a heartbeat? If not, external cardiac massage should be applied. This may be sufficient for adults suspected of having cardiac arrest. For drowning victims and children with respiratory problems, mouth-to-mouth resuscitation may be necessary.

Think first: If the person can talk or cry, he or she is conscious, able to breathe, and has a pulse!

ARTERIAL vs. VENOUS BLEEDING

Arterial bleeding—recognized as being bright red and coming in spurts—must be stopped immediately. Apply direct pressure to the wound. The use of a tourniquet is not recommended unless the person has a massive wound which makes it impossible to control the bleeding with pressure alone. Get medical assistance as soon as possible.

Venous bleeding is darker, under less pressure, and more readily controlled.

SHOCK

Shock is a very common reaction to significant injuries. If a person feels weak, dizzy, sweaty, turns pale or has a weak but rapid pulse, it may well be due to shock. To treat shock:

- Have the person sit, or preferably lie down on a blanket.

- If there is no neck injury, place an unconscious person on his or her stomach and turn the head to one side.

- If the person is conscious and does not have a head wound, place the person on his or her back on a blanket and elevate the feet 12-15 inches.

- Be sure to keep the victim warm.

- Have someone stay near the person for comfort and reassurance.

FRACTURES

Fractures are very common following various types of emergencies. Do not attempt to "straighten out" a broken limb! Call 911 and wait for help. Movement of a badly fractured bone may result in further severe injury. If a simple fracture is suspected, improvise a splint and immobilize the fractured limb. This often reduces pain and prevents further injury.

FIRST AID KIT RECOMMENDED ITEMS

It is imperative that each reader consult with his or her physician regarding the use of any medications recommended in this list. For instance, bismuth subsalicylate (Pepto-Bismol) is commonly taken for upset stomach and general gastrointestinal problems. If you are taking "blood thinner" medications such as coumadin, however, you should not use this medication.

There is no way I can list every possible drug interaction with these recommended items. If there is any question, check with your doctor. Also, if you have children under the age of 12, make sure you have checked with your child's doctor about any medications you may give your child and the recommended dosage.

Most of the recommended medications are available without a prescription. These are known as OTC (over-the-counter) medications:

First aid manual (available at Red Cross)   _____

Band-Aids (many assorted sizes)   _____

Antiseptic/alcohol wipes   _____

Hand sanitizer bottles (2)   _____

Topical antibiotic ointment   _____

Topical hydrocortisone cream   _____

Hydrogen peroxide   _____

Tube of petroleum jelly   _____

Sunscreen   _____

Thermometer   _____

Lighter   _____

Several pairs of latex gloves   _____

Sterile gauze pads, 2-inch (10)   _____

Sterile gauze pads, 4-inch (10)   _____

Sterile roller bandages, 2-inch (5)   _____

Sterile roller bandages, 4-inch (5)   _____

Sterile cotton balls (small pack)   _____

Adhesive bandage tape, hypoallergenic, 1-inch   _____

Triangular bandages (3)   _____

Bandage scissors (EMT scissors)   _____

Maxi sanitary napkins (5) for blood absorption   _____
from major wounds

Irrigating syringe   _____

Ace bandages 2-inch, 3-inch and 4–inch   _____
(2 each size)

Two tweezers (one regular size, one small)   _____

Needle (If you have professional training,   _____
consider including suture material and set.)

Scalpel with extra blades   _____

Pain relievers (non-aspirin pain relievers such   _____
as acetaminophen, ibuprofen, etc.) (Use what you
are most familiar with.)

Bismuth subsalicylate (Pepto-Bismol)   _____
(Check with your doctor for children's dosages.)

Antacids   _____

Stool softeners   _____

Antifungal ointment/cream (e.g. miconazole) _____

Visine eye drops _____

Cough and cold medications (OTC) _____

Diphenhyramine (Benadryl) (This is an _____
antihistamine used for hives, allergic rhinitis, etc.
Check with your doctor for children's dosages.)

Epi-Pen (Learn more at *www.epipen.com.*) _____
If you or a family member is severely allergic to
insect bites or foods, you may need a doctor's
prescription for Epi-Pen.

POISON INGESTION RX:

Syrup of ipecac _____
(Use only if advised by a poison
control center; no longer routinely
recommended.)

Activated charcoal _____
(Use only if advised by a poison
 control center.)

PRESCRIPTION MEDICATIONS
FOR FAMILY MEMBERS

You will obviously need the cooperation of your doctor(s), but I highly recommend that you get extra prescriptions for antibiotics and regularly prescribed medications you or other family members routinely take.

Let your doctor know you are putting together an emergency first aid kit for use in potential disasters and need several months' supply of prescription medicines. Discuss other meds he or she may recommend.

If you wear contact lenses, it would be wise to keep a spare pair (plus contact cleanser bottles) in the first aid kit and get eye medication such as an ophthalmic antibiotic from your doctor just in case!

I hesitate including this information, but I want to make you aware of what is available should the unlikely event of a poison gas attack. Auto-injectable atropine syringes are available for such emergencies. If ever poison gas is used, you need to know about this product. Use requires professional training. Gas masks would also be issued. See *www.fema.gov* for further preparations.

In emergencies, care for your pets may also be a top priority.

CARING FOR PETS CHECKLIST

Check off each item as it is completed:

Write out your plan to care for your pet.   _____

Make sure your pet has proper ID and
up-to-date veterinarian records and vaccinations.   _____

Obtain a pet carrier and leash if you don't have them.   _____

Put pet supplies in a pet grab-and-go bag
if the pet is to evacuate with the family.   _____

Find out which hotels or emergency shelters
allow pets.   _____

Locate pet shelters near the hotel or shelter
where you would most likely evacuate to.
(Remember that most hotels and shelters
will not allow pets!)   _____

IF YOU NEED TO SHELTER YOUR PET

Call your local emergency management office
animal shelter or animal control office to get
their advice and information.   _____

Prepare copies of veterinarian records and
immunizations to leave with the shelter.   _____

Have a backup plan because the shelter   _____ closest to you may also be affected by the disaster.

FEMA GUIDELINES FOR LARGE ANIMALS

1. Ensure that all animals have some form of identification.

2. Evacuate animals whenever possible. Map out primary and secondary routes in advance.

3. Make available vehicles and trailers needed for transporting and supporting each type of animal. Also make available experienced handlers and drivers. It is best to allow animals a chance to become accustomed to vehicular travel so they are less frightened and easier to move.

4. Ensure that destinations have food, water, veterinary care, and handling equipment.

5. If evacuation is not possible, animal owners must decide whether to move large animals to a shelter or turn them outside.

SAFETY OF FAMILY COMES FIRST

The whole subject of pets is highly emotional for many families. My only admonition is not to place the safety and health of the pet(s) above the well-being and safety of the family members. Evacuating the family with pets may greatly complicate matters. If so, the wise approach is to place the pet in a shelter.

PART THREE

THE UNIQUE ROLE OF THE CHURCH

THE TRUE CHURCH: A FORCE IN THE EARTH

I remember hearing the story of a man who was walking along with his brother in a dark alleyway. They came across a man lying in a drunken stupor. The man was dirty, smelled of vomit, and could not walk without support. The older brother helped the man to his feet and, putting his arm around him, he guided him toward a homeless shelter. The drunken man turned his head, looked up to the older brother, and asked, "Are you Jesus?"

And who knows but that you have come to royal position for such a time as this?"

> —Esther 4:14

You are the salt of the earth....You are the light of the world.

> —Matthew 5:13,14

Decisions determine destiny.

> —Ward R. Williams, my father

CHAPTER 8

FOR SUCH A TIME AS THIS
THE UNIQUE ROLE OF THE CHURCH

"For such a time as this." "Salt and light." Very familiar concepts. Many Christians sense we are living in a critical time of world history. For every generation since Jesus was on this earth, however, it has always been important to be "salt" and "light" to those who do not know Him. I want to be like the sons of Issachar, *"who understood the times and knew what Israel should do."* (1 Chronicles 12:32).

The Bible clearly states that Jesus will return someday to earth and reward those who believe in Him with eternal life. This belief has at times hindered some Christians from taking practical steps for disaster preparedness, believing God will spare them such tragedies. This mindset is not wise and is not consistent with the wisdom taught in Scripture nor is it consistent with an understanding of history, biblical, or secular.

The Bible also states graphically that there will be troubles on earth prior to His return. The worst of these times is known as Jacob's Trouble or the Great Tribulation. Prior to the events of Jacob's Trouble, there will be a period of wars, famines, diseases, earthquakes, and other disasters. The duration of these problems leading up to the Great Tribulation is not known.

No one knows the exact timing of the return of Jesus. Many followers of Jesus believe we are in the period of time leading up to the Great Tribulation. The biblical analogy is that of a woman giving birth. A characteristic of labor is that the contractions gradually get closer together and their strength intensifies. Many people sense the problems that the world is experiencing are becoming more frequent and are of a greater magnitude than ever before. While the Bible is silent as to the exact timing of His return, it admonishes everyone to be prepared for His coming.

THE ESSENCE OF BEING A FOLLOWER OF JESUS

The call to preparedness, however, is not primarily because of looming storm clouds. It lies at the very core of what it means to be a follower of Jesus. As a father, I have a biblical responsibility toward my wife and family. Not to care and provide for them is to be worse than an unbeliever. We are to be "salt and light" in this world. We are to be "Good Samaritans" to our neighbors. We are to love our neighbors as we love ourselves. We are to treat others as we would want them to treat us.

When filled with the love of Jesus and the Spirit of God, believers have answers to the heart cries of people who are hurting spiritually as well as physically.

TSUNAMI FAITH

As a physician I have been present during times of severe illness, including the last moments of many people's lives. In times of crisis, the hearts of people are often open to the love of God. In Indonesia, a man was broken-hearted as he saw his wife die after the tsunami in 2004. This man accepted Jesus into his life and received life-changing comfort.

THE NIGHT BEFORE ETERNITY

When I was in medical school, I spoke to a patient in his thirties who was dying of cancer. He initially refused to acknowledge his need for any spiritual help, stating that the Bible was just a good moral book, nothing more.

I did not see him for several weeks, being assigned to a different ward. One day I felt I should stop and speak to him about Jesus one more time. I found him critically ill. He could barely speak. He told me he wanted to pray to receive Jesus into his life, and he did! I found out the next morning that he had died during the night.

Most of life's experiences are not so dramatic. St. Francis of Assisi has been quoted as saying that one should witness at all times and occasionally use words.

ANSWERING HEART QUESTIONS

In times of crisis, people often ask the question, "Why?" or "Why me?" People search for a deeper meaning to what has occurred in their lives. Many look to God and the Bible for answers. Christians and the church need to be ready to answer the questions.

GOD USES YOU AND ME

God still speaks to people through the Bible, through others, and directly to individual hearts. God at times has warned people of pending danger. God offers comfort and gives solace to those distressed and hurting. Through prayer, people are often healed physically and spiritually. And God uses you and me to do these things in His name!

LET YOUR LIGHT SHINE

I want to challenge you and your church to prepare for emergencies and disasters that we so often face and in so doing, bring comfort and hope to your community. *"In the same way, let your light shine before men, that they may see your good deeds and praise your Father in heaven"* (Matthew 5:16). **Remember, you are making the Invisible God visible.**

THE MOST EFFECTIVE WAY TO BRING PEOPLE TO JESUS

I have been in medical missions for almost 25 years and have found that one of the most effective ways to bring people to Jesus is through compassionate ministries. In this chapter I share with you some innovative and unique models. Perhaps one or more of the examples will "speak to you" and inspire you to emulate one or more.

CHRISTIAN COMPASSIONATE MINISTRIES

I will only briefly discuss Christian compassionate ministries that are not tied directly to an individual church. The thrust of this book is to challenge individual churches to develop a compassionate ministry, no matter how small. I am not speaking of church denominations. Many denominations have wonderful national and international compassionate ministries as part of their mission structures. I am speaking of each and every individual church.

Effective large Christian compassionate ministry organizations include World Vision, Samaritan's Purse, Feed the Hungry, Feed the Children, Kingsway Charities, Operation Blessing, Second Harvest, Feed the Nations, Catholic Relief Agency, and hundreds more. Look up the member list of the National Voluntary Organizations Active in Disaster (NVOAD) to get an inkling of how many are involved. (See *www.nvoad. org* and Appendix M.) You may wonder why I did not list the Salvation Army, which has an official role in every major disaster relief effort in our nation. The reason is because the Salvation Army is actually a church denomination. They do a great work!

CHALLENGE TO EVERY CHURCH

Churches should take a leading and unique role in disaster preparedness. Even small or average-sized churches can develop a compassionate ministry. I challenge every church to at least develop their own store of food and clothing to meet the needs within their own congregation.

The lack of preparedness within our nation puts our entire local and national disaster response plans and capabilities at risk of being overwhelmed as we saw during the Katrina disaster. My contention is that the churches can and should play a significant role in increasing the percentage of people who are prepared physically and spiritually.

CHURCHES AT THE CENTER OF PREPAREDNESS: WHY AND HOW

1. Inspire trust. Churches provide a social setting in which many people come to know and trust each other. Even in the larger churches where people may not know each other, they will have a tendency to have more trust in someone attending the same church.

2. Provide frequency of contact with others. Sundays may be the only time a large number of the members will gather, and the church becomes a setting where dissemination of information, education, and training about disaster preparedness could be accomplished. Most people would not take the time to prepare for disaster due to the time and effort required. Doing this at church would be particularly helpful for those who work long hours and for single-parent families, the elderly, and other special needs individuals.

3. Utilize volunteer leadership. A "transformer" (see Chapter 9) can spearhead this effort and take the load off pastoral staff, which is usually over-burdened and may not be the best to lead the preparedness effort.

Members of the church who specialize in disaster response can share valuable information and training with the other church members.

4. Identify special-needs parishioners. Plans can be developed to assist those with special needs in times of emergencies, particularly if their family or neighbors are not able to meet the needs.

5. Establish compassionate ministries. Churches should establish a food pantry and clothing storage area for the needy within their own congregation and be available to their community as needed. If there is not a great need within your church, collect these items and network with other congregations that have greater need or who distribute goods to other ministries.

6. Function as community shelters. In times of emergencies and disasters, churches are often used as community shelters. Church buildings offer more restroom facilities and often have some type of kitchen. If the church also has food and clothing stored, these supplies can be utilized during emergencies.

7. Provide comfort and spiritual help. During times of disaster, churches are a logical place for many people to seek solace, comfort, and spiritual help.

8. Network with community disaster response efforts. Churches that participate in preparing their congregations for disasters will have established relationships within their community and be able to respond in a coordinated way with local emergency agencies. This will be a great benefit to the community as well as a great testimony for the Lord.

9. Teach members to share their faith. The pastoral staff can teach people to share their faith in times of crisis. Hope Force, Int'l trains church members how to be first responders (www.hopeforce.org).

10. Take an active role in cooperation with local disaster response organizations. Churches that take a more active role in disaster preparedness can develop formal relationships with local Emergency Operation Centers, Citizen Councils, NVOAD, and FEMA. This development of relationships before disasters occur will greatly enhance the effectiveness of involving spontaneous volunteers who always show up to help. Often volunteers are not effectively used due to the lack of preparation.

11. Cooperate with other compassionate ministries. Informal networks of churches that have been working together during times when no disaster is present will be much more effective through their combined efforts in times of disaster.

Two examples of smaller congregations that have greatly impacted their communities may inspire your church to develop similar outreaches.

ANCHOR BAPTIST CHURCH
PISGAH FOREST, NORTH CAROLINA

Randy Barton has pastored this Missionary Baptist congregation for 23 years. In 1985 the church began a food bank to meet local needs, particularly of the elderly.

When Hurricane Hugo hit North Carolina in 1989, Anchor Baptist responded to the call for relief workers. This started Anchor Baptist on a path of compassionate ministry that has grown steadily ever since.

In 2006, they built a 17,500-square-foot modern warehouse that doubles as a disaster shelter, with hot water pipes underneath to keep the floors warm. This warehouse can shelter hundreds of people at one time and has its own generator and water source as well as good bathroom facilities.

Most recently, the church has delivered many eighteen-wheeler truckloads of supplies to victims of Katrina. This is still ongoing.

Anchor Baptist has long ago shifted from just meeting local needs to being a hub to supply many other ministries and churches with basic relief supplies.

When I went to interview Pastor Barton, I was met by an energetic, jovial, gray-haired man named Tom Willis, who was busily moving pallets of donated supplies. I found out he volunteers more than 40 to 50 hours each week. I also learned that he is 79 years old. And here is the "kicker"; he does not even attend Anchor Baptist Church! He just solidly believes in what they are doing and wants to help.

Types of assistance provided by Anchor Baptist include:

- **Meal Care Boxes** prepared for families contain food supplies that require no refrigeration or heating (for a family of four for two days).
- **Clothing Care Boxes** include shoes and various size clothing for adults and children.

- **Kid Care Boxes** include toys and fun items.

- **House Care Boxes** contain supplies needed to help families repair their homes after a disaster.

- **Personal Care Boxes** include personal hygiene and grooming items and some OTC medications.

- **Baby Care Boxes** contain diapers, formula, and baby food.

- **Clean Care Boxes** are filled with cleaning supplies to help in post-disaster cleanup.

One incredible asset the church has used in times of disaster is their WGCR-AM radio station. This is a 25,000-watt station that normally broadcasts from daylight to dark and piggybacks with the much larger station out of Chicago, WGN. Under FCC rules, in times of emergency, the station is permitted to broadcast 24/7. When broadcasting at night during times of disaster, the signal from the smaller WGCR actually overrides WGN locally.

Several years ago we had major flooding in our area from all the rains associated with Hurricane Katrina. I shared with you earlier about not being able to get out of our home area except over some mountain back roads.

During that time, Pastor Barton kept the station operating around the clock. For many, it was the only link for certain emergency situations.

The radio station has generator back-up for the transmitter and studio as well as another back-up for the studio. They also have a mobile satellite studio if needed. This is a great resource during times of major disasters.

In addition to relief supplies, Anchor Baptist mobilizes relief crews. The names of the crews are self-explanatory:

- **Family Box Crew** involves people in collecting and packaging the various care boxes.

- **Chain Saw Crew** involves men skilled in handling chainsaws and are equipped with safety gear and tools to enter a storm situation.

- **Clean-up Crew** involves men comfortable with lifting and debris removal.

- **Carpentry Crew** primarily secures houses with shingles or part of the roof blown away and do not make permanent repairs.

- **Heavy Equipment Crew** consists of experienced drivers and machinery operators.

- **Transportation Crew** consists of those able to load and transport relief supplies to a disaster area.

Pastor Barton has obtained letters from FEMA, recognizing his church as a valid volunteer relief agency. These types of recognition before disasters occur are vital to rapid deployment of volunteers when emergencies arise.

The network Anchor Baptist has developed includes hundreds of churches and compassionate ministries.

The ministry has grown to the point where they have several eighteen-wheelers as well as other trucks, cars and vans involved with distribution of relief supplies and transportation of people during emergencies. The church also has four small airplanes to assist with movement of personnel and emergency supplies. I want to remind you that this outreach is in a very small, semi-rural community. You can do it, too!

EVANGEL WORSHIP CENTER
CONCORD, NORTH CAROLINA

Evangel Worship Center is a small, thriving, church located in Concord, North Carolina. Founded in October, 1994, Evangel began with a handful of people who wanted to be used by God to make a difference.

I called my friend, Pastor Thant McManus, and asked him how compassionate ministries began at his church. He responded by E-mail, and I share with you excerpts (italicized) below:

We formed the church in October and on that Thanksgiving, we shared the love of God with our neighbors by providing enough food for about 1000 meals. Turkey, vegetables, all the trimmings, were handed out family by family, always with a smile and an offer to pray right then and there for God to come and make the difference that only He can make.

The event was so successful that the next month at Christmas, we almost doubled the amount of families that we touched with the love of God. Love never fails!

We purchased our first building in 1995 and dedicated a room much like many ministries do, to hold clothing and food for those in our community who told us they needed it.

WORKED WITH LOCAL ELEMENTARY SCHOOL

We found that working through local elementary school counselors and principals, we could quickly locate and offer assistance to those who had the greatest need. The teachers see everyday the impact of lack in the lives of our children. We used them as our eyes and ears. We began to put together back-to-school projects, collecting backpacks and filling them with necessary supplies, buying shoes and other new clothes for the school year also gave us favor in our city and community.

WORKED WITH DEPARTMENT OF SOCIAL SERVICES

We learned to work with the Department of Social Services, becoming a resource for the clients who count on others to help make up for their financial shortfalls.

All the while, we felt God's smile upon us.

GIVING FILLS EMPTY PLACE IN ALL OF US

I would feel a strong unction from the Lord to preach sermons about the empty place God creates in all of us that can only be filled when we give to someone in need. The feeling that nothing else will bring comes when we are moved into action by the Spirit of His generosity.

Pastor McManus then told of a mission trip to Haiti in 1997 that revolutionized his church.

1997 HAITI TRIP GREATLY IMPACTED CHURCH

This trip was another key for Evangel because it opened the eyes of our church to what was happening in other places. We took 25 adults on that trip which was almost half the congregation. It shaped the core of the Church into a committed group of evangelists who wanted to go to the uttermost parts of the world with the saving message of the Gospel of Jesus Christ.

WORKED WITH FEED THE CHILDREN IN 1999

Thant and another man in his church responded to a disastrous tornado that devastated Moore, Oklahoma, in 1999 by working with Feed the Children. Through this relationship, Evangel Worship Center began to receive offers of many donated food supplies. The only challenge was that Evangel had to have trucks to be able to pick up the donations!

WAREHOUSE AND TRUCK NEEDED

The church elders rented a 3,000-square-foot facility and obtained a small truck. Quickly they discovered that the donations required larger facilities and larger trucks. Again the church stepped out in faith and purchased a used eighteen-wheeler tractor trailer rig. After refurbishing the rig, one of the first loads was 48,000 pounds of sweet potatoes. It took only three days to distribute this huge load to hungry people in need.

Pastor McManus added in his E-mail:

All of this happened while our Church had about 100 adults and an equally small budget to work with. We learned that if we were able to do something without God's help, He probably was not interested in it.

In 2002 we moved to our current facility, it is a converted 60,000-square-foot warehouse with pallet racks and forklifts. We use part of the building for our sanctuary, classrooms, and offices and part to store our aid.

We send out multiple short-term teams now each month, one or two teams is going into places like China, Haiti, Mexico, Guatemala, Macedonia, Africa and numerous others. We outfit teams from other Churches and ministries with items from our warehouse, helping to send them to the ends of the earth with God's love. These items range from low-tech bandages to high-tech medical equipment, medicines, food items, clothing, and educational materials.

COMMON CHARACTERISTICS OF FIRST TWO MODELS

1. Both are small churches, about one hundred members. Anchor Baptist is in the small community of Pisgah Forest, North Carolina and Evangel Worship Center is in a suburb of Charlotte, North Carolina. You do not need to be a big church to make a big impact.

2. Both started small and the outreaches just grew naturally to meet the expanding opportunities to minister to those in need.

3. Both have established local community relationships as well as national compassionate ministry relationships.

4. Both ministries have been recognized by local, state, and national governmental agencies.

5. Both have been designated to fill particular niches in relief work and disaster response in their local communities.

6. Both have become a hub and provide food, clothing, and supplies for other churches and ministries.

7. Both provide supplies to teams that address international needs as well as relief work in the U.S.

8. The Gospel is shared with those they help physically, whenever possible.

DENOMINATIONAL EXAMPLES

Many church denominations have developed extensive compassionate ministry arms within their organizations, both nationally and internationally. For purposes of illustration, I will only share two of them. I am including this information just to remind you to look to your own denomination for other volunteer opportunities and perhaps support of your own church's efforts.

SOUTHERN BAPTISTS

Southern Baptists have one of the most vigorous disaster relief programs I have seen in any denomination. Coordinating and tracking over 30,000 volunteers is done through a sophisticated computer program. The certifications of each volunteer are kept on record for skills such as basic life support, advanced life support, first aid, approval to operate chain-saws, etc.

Their national mobile kitchen program can feed hundreds of thousands of people when fully mobilized. In addition, their program is well coordinated with governmental disaster response agencies such as FEMA. If you are a member of the Southern Baptist Convention, I recommend that you consider volunteering through their program.

ASSEMBLIES OF GOD

Having been the founding director of the medical mission program of the Assemblies of God HealthCare Ministries from 1983 to 1994, I am very familiar with their programs. While my involvement personally focused on the international medical mission programs including disaster relief efforts, the Assemblies of God has a broad-based compassionate ministries program in the U.S. at the national headquarters level.

MAPS (Mission America Placement Service) workers have a group of volunteers known as the "RVers" who travel around the nation and provide assistance to churches and ministries in the areas of construction and rebuilding following disasters such as tornadoes, flooding, or hurricanes.

Convoy of Hope is another major compassionate ministry arm that has focused on food distribution in non-emergency times and also relief supplies following disasters. Local churches often invite a Convoy of Hope to come to their area.

Teen Challenge, the well known program ministering to people with various addictions, is an organization of the Assemblies of God.

INDIVIDUAL CHURCH
COMPASSIONATE MINISTRIES

It is estimated that over 130,000 churches in the United States have some type of social outreach activity headed up by volunteers. Is your church one of them? I hope this book will spur you to expand whatever you are currently doing through your church.

CHALLENGE TO LARGER CHURCHES

The examples shared have been about smaller churches getting involved in compassionate ministry. But I also want to challenge those who may be members of much larger churches.

The Dream Center in Los Angeles, California, has one of the largest social outreach programs that I am aware of. The Dream Center was started by Pastor Tommy Barnett from First Assembly of God, Phoenix, Arizona. His son, Matthew, heads up more than 250 programs in operation at the Dream Center, including programs for drug addicts, prostitutes, gangs, alcoholics, the homeless (including teens), and other specialized ministries.

This would not be possible without many churches and organizations and individuals joining hands, but I want to point out that the vision was given to one man at one church and has resulted in impacting thousands. I'm sharing this story to challenge you to do whatever the Lord may place on *your* heart to do.

THE TRUE CHURCH

Let's not forget—you and I are the true church. Believers. The church is not a physical building or a denomination. You have heard it said, "The only Jesus most people will see is you."

I want to repeat the story I shared at the beginning of this chapter.

I remember hearing the story of a man who was walking along with his brother in a dark alleyway. They came across a man lying in a drunken stupor. The man was dirty, smelled of vomit, and could not walk without support. The older brother helped the man to his feet and, putting his arm around him, he guided him toward a homeless shelter. The drunken man turned his head, looked up to the older brother, and asked, "Are you Jesus?"

This experience had such an impact on the younger brother that he entered full-time ministry.

GOOD WORKS

In my experience with many different Christian organizations, I have observed that individuals can at times get lost in the promotion of institutions and the work they do. The Bible says, however, that we are to do our good works in such a way that God receives the glory. If done right, people will sense that it is the love of God in our hearts that compels us to help them.

INSTITUTIONALIZED COMPASSION

You have heard the statement, "I gave at the office," when someone is asked to contribute to a charity. Some people feel if they have given money to a cause, no more is required of them. They somehow feel exempt from personally involving themselves with a needy person close by.

I cannot tell you strongly enough that no institution has an ounce of compassion. Only you and I do. We need to let the compassion of Jesus work through us. As James says, when we see someone naked, hungry, or cold, we do not just say to them "God bless you." We give them the practical things that they need.

LOVING OUR NEIGHBOR

Jesus very clearly taught that we are to love our neighbor in the same way we love ourselves. We are to do for others the things we would want them to do for us. Jesus said if we do that, we will be fulfilling all that the Scriptures ask of us.

To love God is to love others.

GOOD DEEDS ARE NO BENEFIT TO YOU WITHOUT LOVE

Even if we help others, all of our good deeds will amount to no benefit to ourselves unless we do these good deeds with love.

*If I speak in the tongues of men and of angels, but have
not love, I am only a resounding gong or a clanging cymbal.*

*If I have the gift of prophecy and can fathom all mysteries
and all knowledge, and if I have a faith that can move
mountains, but have not love, I am nothing.*

*If I give all I possess to the poor and surrender my body to
the flames, but have not love, I gain nothing.*

*Love is patient, love is kind. It does not envy, it does not
boast, it is not proud*

*It is not rude, it is not self-seeking, it is not easily angered,
it keeps no record of wrongs.*

Love does not delight in evil but rejoices with the truth.

*It always protects, always trusts, always hopes,
always perseveres.*

Love never fails.

−1 Corinthians 13:1-8

Remember—God is love!

WHO? ME?

It is important to know that God "qualifies the called," not necessarily "calls the qualified."

For the eyes of the Lord range throughout the earth to strengthen those whose hearts are fully committed to him.

—2 Chronicles 16:8-9

So I sought for a man among them who would make a wall, and stand in the gap before Me on behalf of the land, that I should not destroy it.

—Ezekiel 22:29-30 (NKJV)

CHAPTER 9

TRANSFORMERS
VOLUNTEER LEADERS WITHIN THE CHURCH

Do you realize that almost every leader called by God in the Bible was reluctant to accept the call? Moses told God six times, "I don't want the job!" But he was the man for the task. Jeremiah said he couldn't do what God was asking him to do. Still in his teens, Jeremiah responded, "I am only a child!" Gideon had to be reassured with miraculous signs before he accepted the challenge of fighting the Midianites. Is God calling you to be the *transformer* in your church?

You may well protest that this should be the job of your pastor or ministerial staff. This most often is not the case. You need to be aware that many pastors are over-burdened and are not in a position to take on one more major responsibility. Possibly your pastor may not feel best qualified to take the primary leadership role in such an endeavor. Your pastor may recognize the importance of having a compassionate ministry and disaster preparedness program and would welcome someone to assume the role of "transformer" or "champion" to develop such a program. It is to such potential "transformers" and "champions" that I am directing my attention in this chapter. As you read, ask, "Am I the one, Lord?"

I challenge you to consider taking a leadership role in spearheading the effort to develop a disaster preparedness program. I challenge you to be a "transformer," a "champion" to lead the way.

If these words strike a responsive chord in your heart, first pray about it and then discuss it with your pastor and church leadership. Share this book with them. It will help them to better understand the urgency and impact of a compassionate ministry.

Perhaps you are sensing that there is a real need to develop a compassionate ministry within your church, but you are certain you are not the person to lead the program. It may be that God is calling you to be an Aaron—someone who comes alongside another person (Moses) who has the primary call of leadership. You may become the catalyst and not the actual leader.

I would, however, caution you about going to someone else if it is YOU that the Lord is speaking to about taking on this responsibility. He will equip you for the task if He has called you to the task.

You may be feeling uncomfortable with thinking of yourself in terms of being a "transformer" or "champion." Yet our goal as believers is to transform our own lives and way of thinking to conform to the will and purposes of God. It is also our hope and desire to lead others into these truths.

> *Therefore, I urge you, brothers, in view of God's mercy, to offer your bodies as living sacrifices, holy and pleasing to God — this is your spiritual act of worship.*
>
> *Do not conform any longer to the pattern of this world, but be transformed by the renewing of your mind. Then you will be able to test and approve what God's will is — his good, pleasing and perfect will.*
> —Romans 12:1-2

MAKING YOUR LIFE COUNT

Within the heart of many people is the desire to make a difference in the world. Psychologists call this "the desire for significance." We want our lives to count.

Have you ever thought about the fact that when someone loves you, it gives you a sense of "significance" or value? At least to that person, your life "counts"!

Now think about the fact that God loves you. Jesus loved you enough to die for you. This means your life is of infinite value.

You know John 3:16. You probably can quote it:

> *For God so loved the world that he gave his one and only Son, that whoever believes in him shall not perish but have eternal life.*

I am always amazed at the fact that the Creator of the universe wants me to be His son and that He knew me before I was even born!

> *For You formed my inward parts;*
> *You covered me in my mother's womb .*
>
> ....
> *My frame was not hidden from You,*

When I was made in secret,
And skillfully wrought in the lowest parts of the earth.

Your eyes saw my substance, being yet unformed.
And in Your book they all were written,
The days fashioned for me,
When as yet there were none of them.

—Psalm 139:13, 15-16 (NKJV)

Also consider what the Lord spoke through Jeremiah:

"For I know the plans I have for you," declares the Lord,
"plans to prosper you and not to harm you, plans to give
you hope and a future."
—Jeremiah 29:11

Just as Esther was called for "such a time as this," so you may be called into this leadership role at this important time. Your decision could affect many lives and families.

You may be readily responding to this challenge. If you are, yet are having second thoughts due to a sense of inadequacy, be willing to ask the Lord for his wisdom and strength. Remember what Pastor McManus said:

"All of this happened while our Church had about 100 adults and
an equally small budget to work with. We learned that if we were able to do
something without God's help, He probably was not interested in it!"

It is important to know that God "qualifies the called," not necessarily "calls the qualified." Note what is written in 1 Corinthians 1:26-30:

Brothers, think of what you were when you were called.
Not many of you were wise by human standards;
not many were influential; not many were of noble birth.

But God chose the foolish things of the world to shame the
wise; God chose the weak things of the world to shame the
strong.

He chose the lowly things of this world and the despised things — and the things that are not — to nullify the things that are, so that no one may boast before him.

BE WILLING TO BEGIN

Note that the vast majority of compassionate ministries at churches are run by volunteers. If the program becomes large enough, it may be necessary to add staff. Be willing to start off small, but be willing to begin!

It may well be true that those with the most experience in disaster preparedness may not be the best to actually design and carry out the plan for the program. They may be best utilized as part of a planning committee and participate in teaching and training sessions.

The qualities of the person needed to spearhead a disaster preparedness program are:

- A sense of purpose and "calling"

- Administrative and organizational skills and a sense of how to pull a team together

- Working closely with your pastor and church eldership and a willingness to "come under authority"

- Servant leadership

DEVELOPING A COMPASSIONATE MINISTRIES/ DISASTER PREPAREDNESS PROGRAM

If you have responded to my challenge and have the necessary pastoral and eldership approval to do so, I want to give a skeletal outline of the steps to develop the disaster preparedness program. I am writing with the assumption that no compassionate ministry program has yet been instituted in your church.

FIRST STEPS

1. Ask each volunteer to read this book for baseline information.

2. Form a planning committee. Do not accept just anybody who volunteers to help, but prayerfully select those you feel will be committed to see the project through. Select some who have expertise in disaster planning, if available. If time is a factor, ask them to function in an advisory capacity and review your plans with them.

3. Designate a room or area in the church where donated items can be safely stored.

CLOTHING DRIVE

1. Start a clothing drive. Specify in writing what you need to be donated in as much detail as possible and distribute to the church members.

- Assign someone to take primary responsibility for the clothing drive if you are not going to take the lead in this area.

- Develop guidelines and priorities for how your church members and community members may access this resource.

- Set specific times when donations will be received, and assign a person to make sure the items are stored and categorized appropriately.

- Set specific times when the "clothing store" will be open to allow individuals to choose items. Post these times in a conspicuous place and/or publish in the church bulletin. Someone needs to be designated to oversee distribution of clothing whenever the "clothing store" is open. In emergencies, have someone responsible and authorized to distribute to the person or family in need.

- Accept only donations of clothing that are new or "like new" and that you or a family member would be willing to wear. Instruct people to wash, press, and fold items before bringing them to the church. If the clothing has been worn and needs to be dry-cleaned, have this done before you receive the donation.

- Keep adult and children's clothing separate. Sort clothing according to size (label).

- Find out what other churches are doing in your area. Donate excess clothing items to churches that are functioning as clothing distribution hubs for other ministries, Salvation Army, Goodwill, or other similar agencies.

- Keep your congregation informed when you need more clothing donations.

- Share with the congregation good stories about people who have been helped. Be sensitive about sharing names if it would be an embarrassment to the individual or family.

INTERNATIONAL CLOTHING DONATIONS

If you send clothing in response to international disasters, be aware that a number of countries will not allow used clothing. The reason for this is that in the past, people have often sent old, worn, and unsorted clothing. I have known of container loads of donated clothing being buried by bulldozers when the clothing came as a jumbled mess.

FOOD PANTRY

1. Start a food pantry.

- Assign someone to take primary responsibility for the food pantry if you are not going to take the lead in this area.

- Develop guidelines and priorities for how your church members and community members may access this resource.

- Request canned goods and non-perishable items. If you do need fresh food donations due to a specific need, arrange a time and day to receive such donations and have delivery pre-arranged.

- Assign times when donations will be received and designate a person to make sure that the items are categorized and stored appropriately.

- Set specific times when the "food pantry" will be open to allow individuals to choose food items. Post these times in a conspicuous place and/or publish in the church bulletin. Appoint someone to oversee distribution of food whenever the "food pantry" is open.

- Pre-package food-care boxes for use in emergencies. Assign someone to distribute boxes to the persons or families in need.

- Find out what other churches are doing in your area. Donate your excess food items to a church that is functioning as a food distribution hub for other ministries.

- Keep your congregation informed when you need more food donations.

- Share with your congregation stories about people who have been helped. Be sensitive in sharing names if it would be an embarrassment to the individual or family.

DISASTER PREPAREDNESS FOOD DRIVE

Since this program is tied to disaster preparedness, consider staging a non-perishable food drive with the emphasis on long-term storage food items that a family would not often buy except for disaster preparation. There will be families in every congregation who do not have the resources to buy several weeks' or even months' supply of food.

Those families with sufficient financial resources within the church may consider this a vital ministry need and purchase these provisions for other parishioners.

EXPANDING YOUR CHURCH DISASTER PREPAREDNESS

Since only 10-20 percent of individuals consider themselves prepared for disasters, there is a great need for educating and training individuals on disaster preparedness. In Chapter 8, I detail why I think the church should play a major role in disaster preparedness.

The church is an ideal setting to conduct "Disaster Preparedness" programs where there will be education, training, and actual disaster preparation activities going on. Since people live hectic lives and have little spare time, the church can step in and play a vital role.

Weekly church attendance is a part of many people's normal activities. Using church time to learn about and prepare for disasters will not encroach on their busy schedules. It will also provide a much-needed service to the individuals and families of your church. Childcare would make it easier for single parents to attend. Disaster preparation may well benefit your entire community!

HOW TO GET STARTED WITH DISASTER PREPAREDNESS TRAINING
FEMA Facilitators' Guide

Many people do not know where to start and do not have the time to prepare the needed materials to teach disaster preparedness. This is one area in which the government has done an excellent job. You can obtain a free in-depth facilitators' guide, which includes a DVD with many helpful slides (PowerPoint presentations) and handouts that you can give to attendees.

Separate material is geared to different age groups and guides you in presenting the material. FEMA has done all the legwork for you. Take advantage of it!

To obtain your free copy of this material, call the FEMA Distribution Center at (800)-480-2520 or write to FEMA, P O Box 2012, Jessup, MD 20794-2012.

Below I list a number of activities you may consider as part of your church disaster preparedness program.

DISASTER PREPAREDNESS AWARENESS PROGRAM

1. Develop a disaster preparedness awareness schedule. Ask the pastor to address the issue during regular church services. To be the most effective and reach the most people, at least some of the educating and training should be done at whatever services most people typically attend. Post a printed schedule in a number of places around the church.

2. Ask well-known speakers on the topic of disaster preparedness to attract greater attendance. You should be able to secure several people who are directly involved with emergency planning for your area.

3. Obtain appropriate literature and handouts for the congregation. The Red Cross, Salvation Army, and FEMA offer excellent resource materials. Give the websites of the above agencies as well as the others mentioned in this book so people can follow up in their own time at home. Have literature always readily available. Sell books on disaster preparedness in your church bookstore.

4. Schedule special activity nights:

"GRAB-and-GO BAG" NIGHT

Plan "Grab-and-Go bag" occasions when people are taught what items to include in the Grab-and-Go bags for home, cars, and work. On these occasions, have a demonstration bag for each location on hand. If there are certain items that various members would really like to have, attendees could sign up for the items, pre-pay, and place a group order. You may very well get a volume discount.

KIDS' NIGHT

Schedule a "Kids' Night" when parents can bring their children to learn about preparing for emergencies. These programs need to be specifically designed for children. Check out FEMA's excellent animated program especially for children (*www.ready.gov*).

NIGHT FOR HORSES

Announce several "Horse Nights" for discussing the most common disasters experienced in your local area. Distribute handouts on how to prepare and respond to the emergencies.

ZEBRA NIGHT

Plan "Zebra Nights" to discuss the less common emergencies, including terrorism. People will not attend if they do not want to hear about this subject. Topics such as living off the land and self-defense might be considered on this night.

WEEKLY CLASSES

Consider having weekly classes (or whatever frequency works for your church) and use this book or other books as a textbook. Teach the material systematically.

PARTICIPATE IN COMMUNITY DISASTER PLANNING

Assign someone to develop relationships with the disaster preparedness agencies in your area and, when possible, participate in the planning functions. Ask this person to report back to you and/or the pastor on significant matters that should be brought to the attention of the entire congregation.

VOLUNTEERING OPPORTUNITIES

Make your congregation aware of the volunteering opportunities in your local area. Refer to Chapter 11.

IDENTIFY SKILL SETS OF CHURCH MEMBERS

Ask people to sign up, listing the unique skill sets they may have to be used in times of disaster. Look over the list of crews that Anchor Baptist has mobilized. Create an information sheet where people will be able to check off whether they have CPR training, basic life support, advanced life support certification, or Red Cross first aid training. You may find some of your professional resource advisors in your own congregation.

Use your creativity when making this list of possible areas in which people could help. For example, find out if they are experienced with chain saws and available to work on disaster response crews; ask them to indicate if they are available to provide transportation for food distribution or for people with special needs.

IDENTIFY INDIVIDUALS WITH SPECIAL NEEDS

Identify individuals and families who will need special assistance in time of emergencies and disasters. Assign individuals to take responsibility for being "extended family" to those individuals and check up on them should emergencies arise.

MOBILIZE PRAYER TEAMS

I cannot express adequately how much it means to me and team members to have hundreds of people mobilized to pray for us every time we go on medical mission trips. My wife is in charge of organizing and E-mailing updates to the more than 600 members of our Prayer Initiative list. I know this has made a significant difference in each trip. The prayers are felt!

I encourage you to mobilize prayer teams at your church. Pray for our nation and for the Lord to keep His hand on our nation and protect it!

If my people, who are called by my name, will humble
themselves and pray and seek my face
and turn from their wicked ways, then will I hear from heaven
and will forgive their sin and will heal their land.

–2 Chronicles 7:14

Provide teaching on how to meet the emotional and spiritual needs of people during times of emergencies and disaster, starting with themselves. They need to know about the common post-traumatic stress syndrome. They need to be prepared and also not to be surprised about some of their own emotions during such times.

REPEAT AND REPEAT

The suggestions above are not meant to be all-encompassing nor should you only cover each topic once. Repetition and offering classes multiple times should become a regular part of your disaster awareness planning.

YOUR CHURCH AS A SHELTER

If it is probable or even conceivable that your church facility would ever be used as a shelter during emergencies, ask structural engineers or professional, knowledgeable people within your congregation to examine your building and give recommendations to strengthen the building and prepare it for any "horses" you might anticipate. Make necessary repairs or structural changes.

Your church should consider generator backup capabilities, water purification needs, extra food storage, and possibly some type of cots or bedding. Many churches have made provisions for bedding for youth camps. If not, you will have to decide if it is practical to store such items at the church. Check to see if your church insurance policy covers damages or losses due to the use of the facilities during emergencies. If your church is designated by the American Red Cross as an official shelter, you may be covered under their umbrella policy.

SHARE WHAT YOU HAVE LEARNED

Once you have developed your program, consider sharing what you are doing with other churches. Be willing to send teams to share experiences with them.

Consider conducting a local seminar involving several churches. Depending upon how you plan to conduct the seminar, make arrangements to invite the public. Hopefully, this will be the beginning of establishing new networks between churches.

PART FOUR

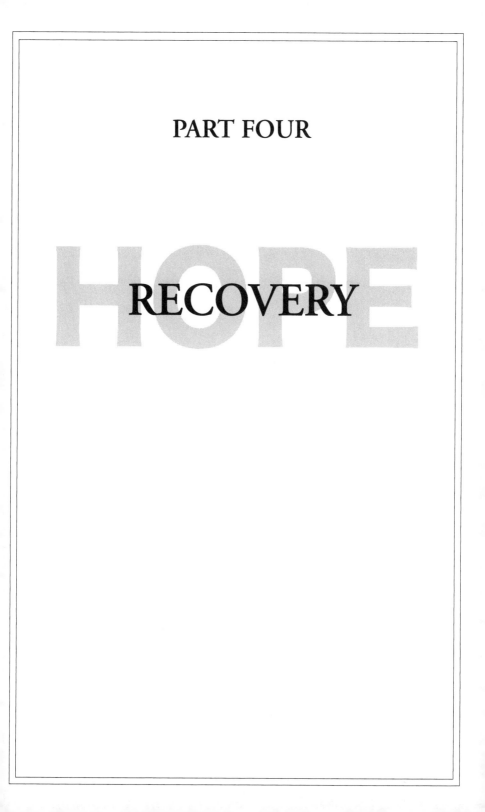

RECOVERY

TOGETHER WE CAN

We must, indeed, all hang together, or most assuredly we shall all hang separately.
                                                        —Benjamin Franklin

(In the Continental Congress, just before signing the Declaration of Independence, 1776)

I can do some things you cannot do. You can do some things I cannot do. Together we can do great things.
                                                        —Mother Teresa

CHAPTER 10

HANG TOGETHER, OR HANG SEPARATELY
INDIVIDUAL AND COMMUNITY RECOVERY

To expect any hope for success during the Revolutionary War, Benjamin Franklin stressed unity. The same applies to recovery from disasters, especially those of the magnitude of Katrina or 9-11.

September 11, 2001 was an infamous day in American history. Yet it was also one of our finest hours. We saw incredible heroism. People from around the U.S. and around the world responded with deep compassion. For the first time in years, there was a pervasive sense that it was OK to be patriotic. People proudly flew the flag of our nation. There was a groundswell of support for the victims' families. Unprecedented!

Many people from all over the U.S. traveled to "Ground Zero" and selflessly gave of their time and resources. The whole nation rallied. We were hanging together as one people. It was an awesome feeling.

In fact, there were so many who were not part of any recognized agency that it forced the government and National Voluntary Organizations Active in Disasters to address ways of managing these spontaneous, non-affiliated volunteers. (See Chapter 13.)

People flocked to churches. It became OK to pray publicly with great frequency. But the sense of unity lasted only a few months.

In times of disaster and emergencies, people tend to set their differences aside and reach out to those in need around them. We should continue to do that as a nation. Believers should lead the way!

Tough times often bring people together. Sometimes it has resulted in getting the Gospel out. China is a good example of how Christians "hung together" and the "Church" grew under the fires of persecution.

Disasters don't just bring out the best in us, however. Looting, vandalism, mob violence, gangs, theft, and intimidation can also be a part of the immediate aftermath.

I will not dwell on these "dark side" issues, but I will address them briefly later in this chapter. Excellent references are available for those wanting more information on securing their home and learning self-defense. The need for such information varies widely, depending upon where you live and the type of disaster you may encounter.

My goal is not to raise fears, which have a tendency to immobilize people. When that happens, they are not able to follow the basic emergency preparedness steps.

FIRST THINGS FIRST

When approaching a railroad crossing, what are you instructed to do? You are told to "Stop, Look, and Listen"! Following disasters, I would like to add the word "Smell." Gas leaks will have a distinctive odor and can easily be detected by smell.

In the immediate aftermath of a disaster:

- Evaluate the health and safety of your family.

- Check for any injuries.

- Do not move any seriously injured person unless he or she is in immediate danger of further injury or death.

PHONE USE

Once your extended family has been notified as to your status, keep phone use to a minimum. During major disasters, keeping the lines of communication open as much as possible for emergency personnel will benefit everyone.

SAFETY ISSUES FOLLOWING DISASTERS

Think "safety." Look for:

- Damaged or exposed electrical wiring
- Gas leaks
- Broken glass
- Contaminated buildings
- Chemical spills
- Slippery floors

If traveling, look for:

- Washed-out roads
- Damaged bridges
- Downed power lines.

As I am writing this chapter, I heard on the news about 1,000 homes being damaged due to floods in the Midwest and over 100,000 homes without power. Another tragedy occurred as a result of this same storm. Three people died in Wisconsin from electrocution when a live wire fell next to them as they were standing in water. A person trying to help them was electrocuted as well and also died.

Remember: Stop and look before helping! As tragic as it was, there were several emergency personnel nearby who recognized they were unable to help and did not try. They did express their emotional pain in feeling helpless in the situation. Refer to Chapter 7 for more information on dealing with basic first aid guidelines.

Once you have determined that everyone in your family is safe, or you have done all you can to assist those who have been injured and made them as comfortable as possible, seek help. Also look around and see if any neighbors need help.

DON'T TRY TO DO TOO MUCH ALL AT ONCE

Following very traumatic events, it is not uncommon to be in a state of shock. Beware of becoming exhausted, both physically and emotionally. Pace yourself. Sit down and evaluate the situation.

"TODAY BE NOT EVERYDAY"

This is another favorite West African saying. In other words, I don't have to get everything done today. Take your time. Pace yourself. Understand that recovery is often a gradual process.

YOUR HEALTH

If your family is relying on you, remember the instructions of the flight attendant to "Put Your Own Mask on First."

- Get plenty of rest.

- Keep well-hydrated with water you know is clean.

- Keep your energy level up by eating well. Another West African saying is, "An empty bag can't stand!" In other words, if your "bag," that is your stomach, is empty, you will be too weak to stand.

- Make sure you dress in clothing suitable for any clean-up required. Wear sturdy boots and good work gloves.

- Be aware of your surroundings.

- If clean-up involves working in contaminated water, be extremely careful to wash your hands thoroughly with soap and clean water frequently. Leave your contaminated clothing outside when you finally do go back into your home or other shelter.

- Shower immediately, if possible.

DEALING WITH ANIMALS, WILD AND DOMESTIC

Wild animals and even domestic animals that are stranded or injured, even your own pets, can be dangerous and unpredictable when they are frightened. Call animal control or your wildlife resource office. If this is not practical, avoid the animal and care for yourself, your family, and neighbors. Trying to help the animal may make you a "victim."

If you have returned to inspect your home, don't corner or approach a wild animal taking refuge in your home. Try to provide some way of escape for the animal, such as an open door or window. If you are bitten, seek medical help as soon as possible.

The concern for animal bites often revolves around the issue of rabies. Vaccination of your animals and livestock will reduce the risk of the spread of rabies, post-disaster. If you are bitten by an animal, if at all possible have the animal available to be tested, if rabies is an issue.

Never handle dead animals. They can be a serious health risk.

PRECAUTIONS TO TAKE WHEN RETURNING HOME

If you have had to evacuate your home and are now returning to inspect for any damages, there are several very important things to do.

Have a battery-powered radio to keep you updated on the current emergency information being broadcast as you return home.

1. Special Precautions with Gas

If you have a battery-powered flashlight, turn it on before entering your home, assuming you have gas in your home. Should there still be power, turning on your flashlight or flipping an electrical switch could cause a spark and an explosion if gas is present.

- Do not enter your home with anything that has a flame, such as a candle or lantern.

- Do not smoke!

- Do not enter your home if you smell gas.

- Have a professional person turn the gas back on in your home.

2. Dealing with Post-Flooding

- Do not enter your home if flood waters remain.

- Have your home inspected and do not enter unless it is declared safe by authorities.

If you feel it is safe to enter:

- Watch for loose boards and slippery floors.

- Be aware that snakes might have entered.

- Follow the guidelines above if a wild animal or even a domestic animal (other than your own) is found in your home.

- Check for sparks and loose wiring.

- Do not touch electrical wiring or electrical switches.

- Do not turn on lights unless you know it is safe to do so. If there is any doubt—don't!

- Do your inspection when you are wearing dry clothing.

- Have an electrician check your house wiring.

- Check for roof, foundation and chimney cracks.

- Check for wet appliances.

- Check your basement. If your water is contaminated and your sewage system backed up, it will present a real health hazard.

- Drink only bottled water or water you know to be pure.

- Food not contained in cans, sealed jars, sealed glass containers, or in other waterproof containers may be unsafe and need to be discarded.

- Open cabinets carefully because objects might fall out.

FEMA has published a 362-page document entitled, "Repairing Your Flooded Home" (Document #234) that gives information on repairing your home. Go to *www.fema.gov/hazards/floods/lib234.shtm*.

Another good resource from FEMA is: "After a Flood: The First Steps," which gives tips on staying healthy, clean-up and repair, and getting help after a flood. Go to *www.fema.gov/hazards/floods/afufld.shtm*.

3. Dealing with Fire Damage

See Chapter 4 and Appendix A for mitigation, preparation, and response to fires.

It is vitally important not to re-enter your home or building unless told it is safe by the authorities.

4. Contact Your Insurance Agent

Regardless of the cause of damage to your home or property or injury to yourself or family member, you will need to contact your insurance agent or agents, depending upon the type of loss you have experienced and the type of insurance coverage.

A word of caution: While it is important to report your injuries and losses immediately, take time to assess everything. Don't settle too quickly. Immediately following a disaster, you may be in shock and not thinking clearly. Most insurance agents may well have your best interests at heart; remember, they are working for the insurance agency and may be under pressure to minimize losses to the company.

If you let several days go by, you will be amazed at how much you might find you have actually lost. Review your records, pictures, and videos of your home and personal belongings before signing off on any insurance settlements.

In addition, following some disasters, there may be federal assistance available.

5. Emotional Recovery Following Loss

You need to know about emotional recovery from significant losses and dealing with psychological stress following traumatic events. You also need to know where to go to get practical help. Hopefully, your church community, family, and friends will be good resources, but it may be necessary to seek additional professional help.

6. Helping Children Cope Following Disasters

One of the best ways of helping children cope with emergencies and disasters is properly preparing them before any disaster occurs.

If the children have participated in the disaster preparedness process, they will have already addressed some of their concerns and fears. Using materials designed for children during the preparation process will be very helpful.

Also, remember, negative responses to disasters and expressions of fear will readily be transmitted to children. Your faith and remaining calm during times of emergency will greatly help your child cope with any disaster—before, during, or after.

Another FEMA publication, "Helping Children Cope with Disasters" (L-196), provides information to prepare children for disaster and to lessen the emotional impact. Go to *www.fema.org/rrr/child.shtm.*

HOME SECURITY/CRIME PREVENTION

Much has changed in our nation. In pioneer days, people would leave their homes unlocked even when they were not home, in case strangers passed through and needed food and shelter.

My wife and I live in a small community. A local, elderly man and his wife ground and packaged various types of flour for pancakes or grits. If they were not home to sell the goods, they left the door open and told people to help themselves and leave the money on the counter. The system worked! (The gentleman recently passed away, and his wife moved to another state.)

Most people do not live in an area where such openness can occur or is even safe or possible. The basic steps to take for your personal home security and crime prevention are the same before and after a disaster.

1. Use Quick Release Locks

Installing security locks on all doors and points of entry to prevent burglary and theft is wise, but be sure they are equipped with quick-release mechanisms in case of fire.

2. Keep Home and Surroundings Well Lit

Keeping your home and surrounding areas well lit at night often discourages would-be-thieves.

3. Where to Leave Keys?

Never leave the keys to your home under the doormat. Select a non-traditional site—away from the door—to store the keys.

4. Night Vision

At night, be very aware of the fact that people can see into your home better than you can see out. Expensive TVs, computers, or other desirable objects may attract thieves. Closing blinds or curtains may be advisable.

5. Home Security Systems

Electronic home security systems are another option. Some friends of mine have a very sophisticated system that is tied into the fire and police call centers as well as the home security company. The more sophisticated the system, the more expensive, of course.

6. Home Security Following A Disaster

The major difference between security for your home before and after a disaster is that it may be much more difficult to secure if there has been widespread damage. In such situations the National Guard, police, and other security personnel often are assigned to patrol affected areas.

7. Neighborhood Watch

Good neighbors look out for each other. (Refer to Chapter 13.) Contact some of the existing networks in your community to find out how they have planned to handle emergency response and disaster follow-up. One of the programs is USAonWatch-Neighborhood Watch, which has expanded beyond their traditional crime prevention. See *www.USAonWatch.org.*

8. Self-Defense

I approach this subject with reluctance since everyone has their own level of comfort with this topic. A few general guidelines are listed below. (See Aton Edwards's book, *Preparedness Now!,* for a more in-depth discussion of this topic.)

SELF-DEFENSE ADVICE

- Avoid confrontation if at all possible. The old saying is: "I'd rather be a live chicken than a dead duck!"

- Particularly after disasters, take some form of protection such as a walking stick, cane, or sturdy umbrella should you encounter stray animals (including human)! This is advisable even in peaceful times as well.

- When walking outside during chaotic conditions following a disaster, do not go alone. While traveling overseas, I have often advised teams to go in groups when they want to shop or take a walk.

- Pepper spray with an SHU (Scoville Heat Unit) number of at least 2 million is recommended. This is a good alternative for those of us not wanting to use any firearms.

USE OF FIREARMS

I do not recommend the use of firearms unless you have been extensively trained by the military or a law enforcement agency. As a physician, I have seen too many people killed accidentally. Children may find the firearms and use them in play with disastrous results. Also, if you are not well trained, it is very possible that an attacker will take your own weapon away from you and use it on you!

Some people say that keeping a shotgun in the home for personal defense is the best choice if one is going to have any such weapon. Just the sight of it may turn a thief into an upright citizen. Shotguns do not require the same degree of accuracy when firing. You can purchase a shotgun much more easily than a handgun.

Don't use a toy gun to scare a would-be attacker. If the attacker has a firearm, he may well use it on you if he thinks (mistakenly) that you also have a gun. If you are going to show a weapon, make sure it is real. Also, do not show a weapon unless you know how to use it and are willing to use it!

MARTIAL ARTS

There are many other ways to defend oneself, such as learning martial arts. I personally have not chosen to go that route.

GUARDIAN ANGELS

I have faced some very dangerous situations over my years as a medical missionary in 105 nations. Just one example is the time another missionary and I were stopped by drunken Nigerian soldiers carrying rifles in a remote area at night.

I also used to walk the streets of Chicago and Los Angeles in my work with teen gangs and drug addicts. I found my best protection was prayer and being led by the Spirit of the Lord. According to the Psalms, we do have guardian angels.

EMERGENCY ASSISTANCE FOLLOWING DISASTERS

Many agencies will provide direct assistance following a disaster. (See Appendix L.)

1. **Your church,** if it has developed a compassionate ministry program, would be an excellent place to start.

2. **The Salvation Army**

3. **American Red Cross** and other organizations also offer assistance.

4. **Federal Assistance Programs**

   The federal government works in cooperation with state authorities and private firms and together offer a range of disaster insurance, loan, and grant programs. The Katrina experience has shown, however, that the assistance may be long in coming and requires much patience and filling out many forms.

   - **Contacting FEMA**

   The Federal Emergency Management Agency can be reached at 1-800-621-FEMA or *www.fema.org.*

   - **Government Disaster Help**

   For information related to disaster management, response, and recovery, go to: *http://www.disasterhelp.gov.*

   - **Federal Citizen Information Center (FCIC)**

   For questions about federal agencies, programs, benefits, and services, call 1-800-FED-INFO (1-800-333-4636).

- **National Flood Insurance Program**

See Chapter 6 for details about the National Flood Insurance Program. For further information, go to: *www.floodsmart.gov/floodsmart/pages/index.jsp.*

The NFIP is a cooperative effort between the federal government and private insurance companies.

- **Home Mortgage Insurance**

If your home was destroyed or significantly damaged by a presidentially-declared natural disaster, you may be eligible for home mortgage insurance offered through the Department of Housing and Urban Development (HUD), working through approved lenders.

- **Small Business Disaster Relief Loans**

If you have a small business that was impacted by a presidentially-declared natural disaster, you may qualify for a disaster relief loan through the Small Business Administration.

Contact information for the SBA is:

Small Business Administration
409 3rd Street, SW
Washington, DC 20416
(800) 659-2955 Customer Service
www.sba.gov.

- **Federal Assistance to Individual and Households Program (IHP)**

You may be eligible for FEMA grants for housing assistance and other serious needs for disaster-related expenses such as personal property, transportation, medical, dental, or funeral expenses.

- **FEMA Temporary Housing Program**

  o **Mortgage and Rental Assistance Program**
    If you have received notice of eviction or foreclosure

due to financial hardship resulting from a disaster, you may be eligible for assistance.

○ **Rental Assistance**
If your home has become unlivable due to a disaster, whether you are a homeowner or renter, you may apply for rental assistance.

○ **Minimal Repairs Program**
If your home has minor damages but is unlivable as a direct result of a disaster, you may be eligible for money through this program.

● **Disaster Unemployment Assistance**

If you lose your job as a result of a disaster and are not eligible for regular unemployment insurance compensation, you may be eligible for this assistance and receive a weekly subsidy.

● **Emergency Food Coupons**

You may be eligible for food coupons following a disaster based on your need. The U.S. Department of Agriculture and state authorities administer this program.

VOLUNTEERING POST-DISASTERS

The need for volunteers may last for months after a major disaster. Full recovery may take years. Volunteering through your church network or community networks during the recovery phase of a disaster will benefit both you and your community.

Hopefully, your church has already established relationships with different agencies such as FEMA, or the churches you are networking with have already done so. I recommend you try to network with an affiliated volunteer group when working with larger disaster response efforts. This will result in a better volunteering experience for you and more people will be helped.

DONATE MONEY, TIME, AND SERVICES

Find reputable organizations to donate money to help with the disaster recovery. You will note that the larger organizations keep track of their volunteer hours because it shows the value of what they do as an organization.

You may also have specialized skills that you can offer to the recovery efforts. As you share of your money, time, and service, you will find the truth in the words: "It is more blessed to give than to receive!"

PART FIVE

BEING READY

FINISHING WELL

Nothing is particularly hard if you divide it into small jobs.

—Henry Ford

The key is not to prioritize what's on your schedule, but to schedule your priorities.

—Stephen Covey

Do not merely listen to the word, and so deceive yourselves. Do what it says.

—James 1:22

CHAPTER 11

GETTING YOUR ACT TOGETHER
PUTTING YOUR DISASTER PREPAREDNESS PLAN TOGETHER

Signs are wonderful. They are necessary. They are extremely helpful at times. They tell us which way to go or warn of potential hazards. Signs are good.

But have you ever thought about the fact that a sign points the way to go, but never follows it? This is like the man in the book of James who sees his face in a mirror and then forgets what he has seen. Don't be like that man. Don't just read this book and do nothing. Be the wise person who sees the storm coming and actually prepares for it.

Remember the connect-the-dots coloring books? You first would trace the outline of what you were to color by following the numbered dots, and soon an animal or object would appear. In this chapter I will review the action items you need to follow to "connect the dots" and complete your personal and/or family disaster plan.

I recommend you get a **loose-leaf, three-ring notebook** and place each sheet of paper you add in a plastic sleeve. This will allow you to readily enter new information and rearrange the categories as desired. You can also then work on different segments of your plan without worrying about having space for new materials. You may want to have more than one copy of your disaster preparedness plan and keep the copies in different places. For example, you may want to keep one in your home, one at work, and one in your car.

DISASTER PREPAREDNESS PLAN NOTEBOOK

Include all the essential preparedness plans as outlined in this book. I have chosen to list the categories in the order that they were presented, beginning with Chapter 3.

1. Establish a schedule. Set aside time each week for disaster planning— at least one-half hour, although 1-2 hours per week would be better. Include all family members at least once each month. Be sure children are included in age-appropriate ways. Make planning a game for the children.

Do not instill fear!

2. Establish a physical fitness program for yourself and your family. Put it in writing so that each family member can review and monitor his or her progress. Make this a family accountability item and encourage each other to reach desired goals. Becoming physically fit may be a matter of avoiding major injury or even death.

3. Put your nutritional goals in writing, particularly if you have not been routinely eating a healthy diet. Insert several pages of good dietary plans as a reminder.

4. Identify your horses first. Once you have identified the types of hazards you are most likely to encounter, make a **copy of your hazard specific preparedness guidelines**. Insert this information in your notebook. As a family, go over each of the hazards and review, discussing matters at age-appropriate levels. Make sure everyone understands his or her role if specific assignments are given to different family members.

Insert copies of how to deal with the more common disasters where you live. Include other hazards even if you do not specifically run a high risk where you live. Most people travel and may face hazards while away from home.

Place in your notebook all the "Horses" including:

- Fire
- Flooding
- Hurricanes
- Tornadoes
- Thunderstorms
- Extreme cold
- Extreme heat
- Other potential disasters in your area

Be sure to include written instructions for use of generators or other special equipment. Also, list sources for re-supplying fuel for your generator. Remember: In certain crises everyone may be looking for the same items, and you may have to be aware of unusual locations for restocking. This is a good neighborhood action item to discuss. Pooling resources may be an option. Carpooling or biking may become good options for conserving fuel.

5. Make a list of early warning systems available in your community. List the equipment you have to receive these warnings and indicate where they are stored, such as an NOAA Weather radio.

6. Compile an emergency contact list with phone numbers for police, fire, doctor, hospital, schools, electric, gas, and water companies. This list should be inserted in your notebook, beside your phone in the home, in your personal pouch, as well as in each of your emergency kits (personal, home, car, and workplace).

7. Insert evacuation plans and routes determined by local authorities. Include, also, your alternate personal evacuation plans. Planning at least two different routes would be prudent. Include detailed maps and directions. While it is best to follow established evacuation routes recommended by authorities, watching people trying to escape from Katrina on clogged freeways and then running out of gas only reinforces the need for contingency plans.

> **Insert checklist of actions you need to take before leaving home:**
>
> - **Shut off utilities** (electricity, gas, water; include instructions as to where these switches and shut-off valves are located.)
>
> - Include page indicating where the **"Grab-and-Go Bag"** is located.
>
> - **Unplug electrical equipment** (except freezers and refrigerators unless flooding is expected.)
>
> - **Secure home.** Lock doors and windows.
>
> - **Leave note** in a conspicuous place, indicating where you plan to go and how you can be reached.
>
> - **Grab personal pouch** worn under clothing; ideally, the pouch should be pre-packed, except for those items you use everyday and that would most likely already be on your person. Refer to chapter 6 and include in your notebook the **list of items** you have **pre-packed** and then

list items that need to be included at the last minute. Don't forget your cash in small bills!

- **Consider inserting instructions for escaping from a subway,** particularly if this is a frequent mode of travel for you.

- **Include instructions for evacuations from a high-rise building.** This would be prudent even if you do not live in a high-rise. You may need this information at hotels, businesses, or when visiting large cities.

- **Identify where family members should meet** if a disaster hits and family members are in separate areas.

- **Insert copy of school emergency plans.** Be sure the school contact information is readily available.

- **Include copy of workplace emergency plans** and contact numbers.

8. Insert separate lists of what has been included in your **emergency supplies kits** for:

- **Personal**
- **Home**
- **Car**
- **Workplace**

Also indicate in writing where each emergency kit is stored. Include pages with instructions on maintaining your emergency kits.

9. Set up a schedule to rotate food and medications and make sure first aid kits are not outdated.

Include list of foods for long-term storage. Remember to "eat what you store and store what you eat." A minimum of two weeks' food supply is recommended, but many are advocating even 3-6 months' food supply or even longer. **KEEP A LIST** of any perishable foods or stored items with an expiration date and **keep the food supplies updated**.

10. Maintain an updated list of prescription medications for family members. Keep close tabs on expiration dates and set up a rotation schedule. Be sure to include any special handling instructions for medications that may need to be refrigerated.

11. Make a list of all emergency supplies not stored in your emergency kits—items such as extra flashlights, batteries, candles, camping stoves, tents—and indicate where they are stored.

12. Insert basic first aid and CPR instructions. (See Chapter 7.) List the **contents of your first aid kit.** Be sure to create a schedule to review medication or medical supply expiration dates.

13. Include plans for escape routes for fires. Review with family as needed. Copies of escape routes for fires should be posted in every bedroom at eye level for children. Periodically make it a game of "escaping."

14. Include your family communication plans (both immediate and extended family) in the event of an emergency or disaster. Remember to give a copy of these plans to the children's schools. Also, carry this plan in your personal pouch and place in each emergency kit (personal, home, car, and work).

15. Keep copies of medical release forms for each child. It is conceivable that other family members or even friends or neighbors may be responsible for one or more of your children during a hazard. Having this form available to give to responsible adults would be helpful.

16. Include pictures of each family member. (Several copies would be good in case of separation during a crisis.) Make as many copies as you want to store in different sites, including each of the family member's personal grab-and-go bags. You can also scan photos onto a flash drive if you have a computer (as well as other documents) and carry in your personal pouch or emergency kits.

17. Include detailed instructions and plans if you are caring for **individuals with special needs.** Chapter 7 goes into more detail about evacuating if a person with special needs will be accompanying your family.

      If it is impossible to evacuate a special-needs individual for whom you are responsible, be sure to include nursing home or hospital information or emergency contact numbers. Such contingencies should be worked out with the appropriate parties long in advance. The responsibilities of each party need to be clearly understood and stated in writing well ahead of time.

18. Include your plans for caring for animals and pets, taking into account various levels of disasters. List animal shelters and contact information. (See Chapter 7 for more specific information.)

19. Insert any neighborhood preparedness plans, including contact information and any special assistance you or your neighbors have agreed to provide for each other. Keeping a list of each neighbor's resources that could uniquely assist the neighborhood would be helpful.

20. Make copies of appropriate documents you feel should be in your notebook. (Refer to Chapter 6, Appendix E, and Appendix I.) You obviously need to store additional copies (or originals as recommended) in multiple sites. Be sure to **include copies of health, home, auto, and life insurance policies** or at least the account numbers and contact information for each policy. You may scan copies onto a flash drive and then you can reproduce as many copies as you need.

21. Keep copies of immunization records for each family member.

DON'T GET DISCOURAGED!

Putting your personal **Disaster Preparedness Plan Notebook** together may look like too much work. That is why it is important to do a little every week. When you finish, you will have a very personalized notebook that addresses your specific needs. It will be well worth the effort.

ASPECTS OF PREPAREDNESS

For every disaster there are four aspects of preparedness: mitigation, preparation, response, and recovery. As you begin to put your personal plan together, it will become obvious to you what additional preparation will be most advantageous.

Whenever possible, you want to mitigate and prevent disasters. Many "accidents" are preventable. I have come to appreciate the definition of an accident as "a poorly planned event." For instance, a young teenager drag-racing with friends may have an accident, but with better judgment and self-control, it never would have happened in the first place.

MITIGATION IS BEST

I have found that not everyone immediately understands what is meant by the word *mitigation*. Let me illustrate:

My mother used to tell the following story about my older brother, John, when he was quite small. One day my brother decided to walk directly through a wonderfully muddy pool of water. Not only did he get his shoes and clothes wet, but he was also soon covered in mud. My mother scolded him, "Why did you walk through the muddy water and not go around it?" John replied, "It just got in my way!"

If you see the potential for a disaster or emergency that you can avoid by "walking around the muddy pool of water," you have just mitigated the problem. Avoiding and/or minimizing a disaster is wise whenever possible. Don't be in the position of having to say, "It just got in my way!"

Using non-flammable materials to build your home or place of business would mitigate against fire damage. Moving old lumber away from the side of the home mitigates against attracting termites as well as decreases the fire hazard. Getting plenty of rest before taking a long trip may mitigate against falling asleep at the wheel. Losing weight and getting in shape mitigates against becoming a victim in case evacuation on foot becomes a necessity. You get the point. The more you are able to do in the area of mitigation, the less you will have to do in all three of the other areas.

HOME HAZARD HUNT

In her book, *Organize for Disaster,* Judith Kolberg has a great section on mitigation and home hazard hunt. She recommends going through your home and de-cluttering to mitigate against injury and destruction during a disaster.

The better you prepare, the better your response will be should an emergency arise. More often than not, your recovery phase will be shorter and you will have less loss.

WHEN ALL PLANS FAIL

MAINTAIN YOUR STATE OF READINESS

Maintenance is key to excellent preparedness. You may initially plan well for all four steps in each type of hazard, but you may fail to maintain the state of readiness.

For instance, if your food, water, or medications are not rotated and kept up to date, you may not be adequately prepared when trouble arises. If you let insurances lapse, you may not be covered and you may suffer great loss.

Although you are primarily responsible for preparing your family for disaster, I encourage you to take the lead in gathering neighbors together to discuss neighborhood disaster preparedness. You may be amazed at the resources and resourcefulness of your neighbors. You may also find areas of disaster preparedness to add to your notebook.

When it comes time to recover after a disaster, all the neighborhood connections you have been able to forge have the potential of being a great blessing to you.

Some of you will be able to take up the challenge and become "transformers" in your church, helping to develop a compassionate ministry that will benefit your fellow church members and community.

As you become prepared, you are less likely to be a victim. You have a much greater chance of helping others.

HOPE IN TIMES OF CRISIS–DIAL 91:1

The numbers 9-11 instantly bring to mind the destruction of the Twin Towers in NYC on September 11, 2001.

Interesting that when we have an emergency, we are instructed to dial 911.

For believers, we have our own emergency code: Psalm 91:1.

He who dwells in the shelter of the Most High
will rest in the shadow of the Almighty.

Psalm 91 continues:

I will say of the Lord, "He is my refuge and my fortress,
my God, in whom I trust."
Surely he will save you from the fowler's snare

and from the deadly pestilence.
He will cover you with his feathers,
and under his wings you will find refuge;
his faithfulness will be your shield and rampart.
You will not fear the terror of night,
nor the arrow that flies by day,
nor the pestilence that stalks in the darkness,
nor the plague that destroys at midday.
A thousand may fall at your side,
ten thousand at your right hand,
but it will not come near you.
You will only observe with your eyes
and see the punishment of the wicked.
If you make the Most High your dwelling —
even the Lord, who is my refuge —
then no harm will befall you,
no disaster will come near your tent.
For he will command his angels concerning you
to guard you in all your ways;

–Psalm 91:1-11

PART SIX

NATIONAL, STATE AND COMMUNITY EMERGENCY PROGRAMS

IT'S A JUNGLE OUT THERE!

"Where elephants walk, the grass gets trampled" is one of my favorite African sayings. The elephants are the people in positions of power. The grass represents the "little people" with little power. When the big guys throw their weight around, the little guys often suffer. Sadly, I have seen it all too often wherever I have traveled around the world. Such was the case in Rwanda between the Hutu and Tutsi. It is a universal experience.

--Paul R. Williams, M.D.

WHERE ELEPHANTS WALK, THE GRASS GETS TRAMPLED
WHO'S RESPONSIBLE? NATIONAL RESPONSE PLAN

It happened with Hurricane Katrina. I don't have any "inside" information, only what has been printed and broadcast in the news. There are charges and counter-charges between the "elephants," those in positions of authority. There are stories of contractors who knowingly did not meet construction specifications when repairing the levees in order to increase profits. There are stories of graft and greed with billions of dollars handed out by the federal government, and far less actually getting to those impacted by the hurricane than originally intended. Elephants trampling the grass.

My worldview of God's ultimate justice for the poor gives me the hope that someday these injustices will be righted, some on this earth and some in heaven. Justice will be served. I have no envy for those who have taken advantage of the poor. I wouldn't want to be in their shoes when giving account to God for my life. You see, I really do believe that the "good guys" ultimately win!

I do not want to dwell on the negative aspects of elephants. Elephants can't help being big and powerful. That is how they are made. It is how they use their power and strength that is so crucial. I have been impressed with the degree of planning that has been done at all levels of government since 9-11 and Katrina. Efforts to improve the disaster preparedness of our nation can best be described as Herculean. The federal government has led the way through the Department of Homeland Security.

Despite these efforts, there are many detractors that say these efforts will not be enough. I must admit that this is most likely true if, in fact, the statistics are correct that only 10-20 percent of the populace is prepared for disasters. Catastrophic events as great as Katrina will overwhelm any response plan, unless the majority of the people actually take responsibility for their own preparedness. So I'll say it again: "Be prepared. Don't be a victim!"

I emphatically add that in times of emergency, I have found that most people inside and outside of government (local, state, or federal) respond with incredible integrity and heart to do what is right and best for all concerned. The response of Americans to 9-11 and Katrina was heartwarming despite the chaos. It was the chaos that has been the impetus for reshaping our National Preparedness Plan.

If you have never been responsible for organizing a response to disasters, you have no idea how huge the challenges can be when all forms of communication are interrupted, roads are impassable, and the right emergency equipment is not available or has been destroyed. I would advise everyone to be slow to criticize and not be a Monday morning quarterback. You have to have been in the middle of the disaster to appreciate the efforts of the people responsible for coordinating the relief efforts.

I'd like to point out that Hurricane Katrina and its disastrous aftermath represent the single largest natural disaster the nation has ever faced. **Out of this tragedy have come incredible efforts to develop plans to coordinate disasters spanning all jurisdictions—local, state, and federal—and assigning specific roles to different agencies before any emergency actually occurs.**

Despite thorough planning, it will still be a major challenge to coordinate efforts for disasters as large as Katrina.

ELEPHANTS IN INDONESIA

When I was in Indonesia following the tsunami devastation, I saw elephants being used to move heavy debris in several feet of standing water. Modern machinery could not have worked where the elephants were able to work. It was work beyond what individuals were able to do by themselves.

The same can be said for governments. There are some things that can only be done by governments, whether local, state or federal. Sometimes the size, strength, and resources of governments are needed for certain daunting tasks. Depending upon the size and type of disaster, there are laws stating which local, state, and federal governmental agencies are responsible and delineating how they should interrelate.

Local, state, and federal governments' disaster preparedness plans are useful information to keep on hand. The amount of available materials is staggering and beyond the ability and time constraints of most people to digest. As I researched our national disaster preparedness plans, I was reminded of the story of the nine blindfolded people standing around an elephant and attempting to describe the animal.

Another analogy that came to mind was, "I can't see the forest for the trees." As I researched disaster preparedness and the National Response Plan, all I could see were the trees. I believe I can now describe the forest. My research should make it easier to understand the complex efforts needed to respond to major disasters. The following is a "birds-eye view" of what has been planned nationally.

For most people, understanding the disaster response process will help them know what to expect from governmental agencies and how to interface with them in times of disasters.

To carry the analogy of elephants one step further, there are many things an elephant cannot do or cannot do well. There are many things you can do as an individual much better than any government can do, particularly meeting your own unique disaster preparedness needs. In the final analysis when asking the question, "Who's Responsible?" the finger points back at you and me.

Remember, you may well need to provide for yourself and possibly your neighbors for several days before first-responder teams arrive.

In this chapter, however, I am focusing on the role of the elephants—those in positions of authority who bear the responsibility for national safety and defense.

WHAT DOES THIS ALL MEAN TO ME?

The big picture of national preparedness is an area of information that will be of particular interest to those actively involved with disaster relief planning efforts. For me, it was important to understand how the complicated relationships of disaster response are integrated.

I believe this chapter will benefit you in understanding the complexities of managing disasters and, hopefully, cause you to increase your efforts to be personally prepared and not to rely wholly on local, state, and federal responses.

NATIONAL RESPONSE PLAN

After 9-11, the Department of Homeland Security was formed and given broad responsibilities to coordinate national security efforts. One of those responsibilities was to develop the National Response Plan (NRP). It is currently undergoing revisions, but you can access the entire plan at *www. dhs.gov/nationalresponseplan* or obtain a free hard copy or CD by calling the DHS/FEMA Warehouse at (800) 480-2520. If you are involved with local disaster response teams in your community, I recommend that you download the Quick Reference Guide for the NRP and make a hard copy for your records.

Much of the following information is taken from these public documents, interspersed with my comments, to make things as simple and accurate as possible. There are so many agencies and acronyms that I have added Appendix K for a glossary of terms and agencies.

THE NATIONAL RESPONSE PLAN IN A "NUTSHELL"

As required by Homeland Security Presidential Directive (HSPD)-5, the National Response Plan (NRP):

- Establishes a single, comprehensive approach to domestic incident management to prevent, prepare for, respond to, and recover from terrorist attacks, major disasters, and other emergencies. The NRP covers all hazards. The word *incident* refers to any type of emergency or disaster.

- Establishes organizational structures for coordination of many different agencies at the field, regional, and headquarters levels. These organizational structures integrate federal, state, local, tribal, non-governmental organizations (NGOs), and private-sector efforts.

- Addresses both site-specific incident management activities and broader regional or national issues that impact the rest of the country.

- Addresses the immediate regional or national actions required to avert or prepare for potential subsequent events.

- Addresses the management of multiple incidents at one time.

That is the NRP in a "nutshell." As the saying goes, "The devil is in the details."

WHEN IS THE NRP ACTIVATED?

The NRP is always in effect; however, the implementation of NRP coordination mechanisms is flexible and can be scaled up or down according to the need.

The NRP can be partially or fully implemented whether there is a threat, an anticipated significant event, or in response to an incident requiring a coordinated federal response. Coordinated responses will include an appropriate combination of federal, state, local, tribal, private sector, and non-governmental entities.

INCIDENTS OF NATIONAL SIGNIFICANCE

An Incident of National Significance (INS) is an actual or potential high-impact event that requires full coordination of the federal response in order to save lives, minimize damage, and provide the basis for long-term community and economic recovery.

The Secretary of Homeland Security, in consultation with other departments and agencies, and the White House determine when incidents are to be declared Incidents of National Significance. There is no automatic trigger for this designation.

Once an incident has been declared to be an INS, the **Secretary of Homeland Security will manage the federal government's response to the incident**.

ROLES AND RESPONSIBILITIES

A basic premise of the NRP is that incidents should be handled at the lowest jurisdictional level possible. In the vast majority of incidents, state and local resources and interstate mutual aid will provide the first line of emergency response and incident management support. When state resources are overwhelmed, governors may request federal assistance.

NRP AND NATIONAL INCIDENT MANAGEMENT SYSTEM

The NRP and National Incident Management System (NIMS) are companion documents designed to improve the nation's incident management capabilities and overall efficiency. NIMS has been created to provide a consistent framework for managing disaster response.

An incident can be any type of emergency including natural disasters, terrorist attacks, or any other emergency. The NIMS provides the incident management framework at all jurisdictional levels regardless of the cause, size, or complexity of the incident.

Together, the NRP and NIMS integrate the capabilities and resources of various governmental jurisdictions, incident management, emergency response disciplines, non-governmental organizations, and other private sectors.

NIMS IN A "NUTSHELL"

The NIMS structure includes:

- A coordinated plan

- One person in overall command

- One centralized coordinating center that has direct on-scene management responsibilities

- Agreements that are worked out ahead of time as to areas of responsibility for all agencies involved

- Specific guidelines for the coordination of incident management, information, and communication

FEDERAL, REGIONAL, OR FIELD-LEVEL ACTIVITIES

The Department of Homeland Security through FEMA (DHS/FEMA) has regional offices that coordinate regional responses to disasters. These are called Regional Response Coordination Centers (RRCC), and are standing facilities.

When an incident occurs, the RRCC:

- Deploys a DHS/FEMA-led Emergency Response Team—Advance Element (ERT-A), including rapid needs assessment personnel.

- Sends these teams to state operating facilities and incident sites.

- Assesses the situation.

- Gauges federal support requirements.

- Makes preliminary arrangements to set up federal field facilities.

WHEN DHS HEADQUARTERS RESPONSE IS REQUIRED

If the incident overextends regional resources or the event poses potentially significant consequences, DHS Headquarters may:

- Deploy a National Emergency Response Team (ERT-N) to coordinate the initial response.

- Deploy a Federal Incident Response Support Team (FIRST) to the scene to support state operations.

   F I R S T:

   o Provides technical assistance to assess the situation.
   o Identifies critical and unmet needs.
   o Provides recommendations for protective action.
   o Establishes incident support facilities.
   o Coordinates with the ERT-A.
   o Integrates into the Joint Field Office when established.

JOINT FIELD OFFICE (JFO)

When an incident occurs, a *temporary* federal facility is established locally. The Joint Field Office (JFO):

- Provides a central point for federal, state, local, and tribal executives with responsibility for the incident oversight.

- Does not manage on-the scene operations.

- Focuses on supporting on-scene efforts.

- Conducts broader support operations that may extend beyond the incident site.

When incidents impact multiple states or localities, multiple JFOs may be established. In these situations, one of the JFOs will be designated by the Secretary for Homeland Security as the primary JFO.

The JFO organizational structure is built upon NIMS, but does not override the Incident Command Post (ICP) or Incident Command System (ICS) structure, which is directly in charge of on-scene operations. (ICP and ICS functions are discussed in subsequent paragraphs.)

How the JFO is organized is beyond the scope of this book. It is important to note that the structure and planning of the JFO incorporates major federal officials as well as state, local, and tribal officials. The exact composition of the JFO depends on the nature and magnitude of the incident.

Remember: The JFO is set up to coordinate federal support functions for the local or regional incident and will go through the Incident Command Post.

FEDERAL EMERGENCY SUPPORT FUNCTIONS (ESFs)

The areas of federal support have been divided into 15 major areas and are termed Emergency Support Functions (ESFs), which are the primary means through which the federal government provides assistance to state, local, and tribal governments or to federal departments and agencies conducting missions of primary federal responsibility.

I will only list them here, along with the ESF Coordinator. Refer to the *www.dhs.gov/nationalresponseplan* for a complete description.

The ESF structure is modular and only those modules needed in a specific incident will be activated. The names of the ESFs are basically self-explanatory:

ESF # 1 Transportation
Coordinator: U. S. Department of Transportation

ESF # 2 Communications
Coordinator: U. S. Department of Homeland Security/National Communications System

ESF # 3 Public Works and Engineering
Coordinator: U. S. Department of Defense/U. S. Army Corps of Engineers

ESF # 4 Firefighting
Coordinator: U. S. Department of Agriculture

ESF # 5 Emergency Management
Coordinator: U. S. Department of Homeland Security/Federal Emergency Management Agency

ESF # 6 Mass Care, Housing, and Human Services
Coordinator: U. S. Department of Homeland Security/Federal Emergency Management Agency
(The American Red Cross handles the Mass Care element.)

ESF # 7 Resource Support
Coordinator: U. S. General Services Administration

ESF # 8 Public Health and Medical services
Coordinator: U. S. Department of Health and Human Services

ESF # 9 Urban Search and Rescue
Coordinator: U. S. Department of Homeland Security/Federal Emergency Management Agency

ESF # 10 Oil and Hazardous Materials Response
Coordinator: U. S. Environmental Protection Agency

ESF # 11 Agriculture and Natural Resources
Coordinator: U. S. Department of Agriculture

ESF # 12 Energy
Coordinator: U. S. Department of Energy

ESF # 13 Public Safety and Security
Coordinator: U. S. Department of Justice

ESF # 14 Long-Term Community Recovery
Coordinator: U. S. Department of Homeland Security/Federal
Emergency Management Agency

ESF # 15 External Affairs
Coordinator: U. S. Deptartment of Homeland Security

OTHER FEDERAL TEAMS

In addition, there are many special federal teams available to support
incident management, domestic readiness, and recovery operations.

STATE, COUNTY, AND LOCAL
EMERGENCY OPERATIONS CENTERS (EOCs)

State, county, and local EOCs are the physical location where the
coordination of information and resources to support incident management
activities normally take place. EOCs are usually organized by major
functional services (fire, law enforcement, medical services, etc.) or by
jurisdiction (city, county, region, etc.) or a combination of the two.

State, county, and local EOCs facilitate the execution of local,
state, and interstate mutual aid agreements to support on-scene operations.
When activated, the JFO works in coordination with these EOCs to support
incident management efforts.

ROLES OF THE PRIVATE SECTOR

The NRP recognizes the private sector as a key partner in domestic
incident management. For coordination with the owners and operators of
the nation's critical infrastructure, the Department of Homeland Security
and federal agencies utilize mechanisms established under the National
Infrastructure Protection Plan (NIPP), including the Critical Infrastructure
Protection Advisory Committee (CIPAC).

PUTTING IT ALL TOGETHER

So what happens when significant disasters, emergencies, or acts of terror occur? What is the plan of action?

When an incident occurs:

- The appropriate jurisdictional authority (federal, state, or local) designates a single Incident Commander with overall incident management responsibility.

- Most jurisdictions pre-designate their Incident Commander in preparedness plans.

- The Incident Commander directs the operations of the Incident Command Post (ICP), which is usually located at or in the immediate vicinity of the incident site.

- The ICP is the tactical level, on-scene incident command and management organization location.

- The ICP is comprised of designated management officials and responders from federal, state, local, and tribal agencies, as well as private-sector and non-governmental organizations (NGOs).

Most incidents are handled at this level of disaster response. For more significant disasters and emergencies, the Unified Command plan goes into effect.

UNIFIED COMMAND CONCEPT

Unified Command is an application of the NIMS/Incident Command System (ICS), used when there is more than one agency with jurisdiction over a particular disaster or when disasters cross political jurisdictions.

For example, during the response to a bombing, more than one federal, state, or local agency will have jurisdiction. As a team effort, the Incident Commanders from different agencies form a Unified Command. This helps overcome much of the inefficiency and duplication of effort that can occur.

In accordance with the procedures established by Unified Comand, federal, state, and local responders must report to the ICP to receive an assignment, regardless of their agency affiliation. At this point, they are under the tactical control of the Unified Command.

Agencies with jurisdictional responsibilities join the Unified

Command. Agencies that are heavily involved with the response, but without jurisdictional responsibilities, are defined as supporting agencies and are represented in the command structure. Their efforts are coordinated on behalf of their parent agency through a liaison officer attached to the Unified Command.

EMERGENCY OPERATIONS CENTERS (EOCs)

When an incident occurs, the Unified Command notifies appropriate federal, state and local EOCs. The EOCs:

- Coordinate support functions and resources.
- Provide multi-agency coordination.
- Provide communications.
- Dispatch and track resources.
- Collect, analyze, and disseminate information.

Local EOCs notify the state EOCs, which in turn notify the National Operations Center (NOC), one of the elements of the National Response Plan Headquarters.

NRP HEADQUARTERS ORGANIZATIONAL ELEMENTS

There are five major elements in the NRP Headquarters:

- Domestic Readiness Group
- Incident Advisory Council
- National Operations Center (NOC)
- Strategic Information Operations Center (SIOC)
- Principal Federal Officer (PFO)

For more complete information about these elements go to *www. dhs.gov/nationalresponseplan.* I want to make a few points about the National Operations Center elements as they impact local disaster response coordination. The National Operations Center (NOC) links key NRP headquarters components including the former Homeland Security Operations Center.

The National Operations Center (NOC) is comprised of five sub-elements:

- NOC-Interagency Watch (NOC-Watch) is a standing 24/7 interagency organization that fuses law enforcement, national intelligence, emergency response, and private sector reporting. The NOC-Watch facilitates homeland security information-sharing and operational coordination with other federal, state, local, tribal, and non-governmental emergency operation centers.

- National Response Coordination Center (NOC-NRCC) monitors potential or developing incidents and supports efforts of regional and field components.

- Intelligence and Analysis (NOC-I&A) is responsible for interagency intelligence collection requirements, analysis, production, and product dissemination for the Department of Homeland Security.

- National Infrastructure Coordination Center (NOC-NICC) monitors the nation's critical infrastructure and key resources on an ongoing basis.

- Interagency Planning Element (NOC-Planning) conducts strategic level operational incident management planning and coordination.

ACTIVATION OF NRP COORDINATION MECHANISMS

During incidents or potential incidents of lesser severity than an Incident of National Significance, the Secretary of Homeland Security may receive requests for the activation of any NRP coordination mechanism through the NOC.

Remember: Once an incident has been declared to be an Incident of National Significance, the Secretary of Homeland Security will manage the federal government's response to the incident.

DISASTER PUZZLE PIECES

One of the funniest comedy routines I have ever seen is the famous Abbott and Costello dialogue, "Who's on First?" I am told they ad-libbed the entire thing! It is hilarious!

"I Don't Know" was the third baseman. When Abbott responds to Costello's question about who is on third base, Abbott replies, "I Don't Know." Costello then yells in disgust, "Well, if you don't know, then who does? You're the manager!"

Sometimes I feel the same way about disaster relief work and volunteer organizations! Who's on first? The answer often is, "I Don't Know!"

--Abbott and Costello Comedy Routine

WHO'S ON FIRST?
EXISTING NETWORKS

Having been involved in disaster relief work for many years, primarily internationally, I realize the answers are not always easy to come by. What happened after the Katrina disaster pointed out the acute need to clarify roles and responsibilities of the various governmental jurisdictions—local, regional, state, and national. The "elephants" at all jurisdictional levels traded barbs about who was to be blamed for the confusion and chaos that marked the relief efforts.

The revised national Response Plan and National Incident Management System (NIMS) is the U.S. government response to this need as I have outlined in Chapter 12.

The historical Judeo-Christian roots of our nation are the reason why there has been such a strong volunteer base in community services nationwide. In fact, the Bureau of Labor Statistics reported that more than 65 million Americans volunteered in 2005, and the Corporation for National & Community Service CEO, David Eisner, has set a national goal of 75 million volunteers by 2010.

It is gratifying to note that the single largest group of volunteers and NGOs are faith-based, whether providing community services in non-emergency times or during times of disasters!

There are over 200,000 charitable organizations in the U.S. and 81 percent—an estimated 174,000 organizations—use volunteers. This number does not include almost 400,000 small charities, which are almost all run by volunteers.

It is estimated that over one-third of churches in America (an estimated 129,000) have social outreach activities managed by volunteers. It is also estimated that 83 percent of the nation's 380,000 congregations have some type of social service community development or neighborhood projects. The role of churches can be greatly expanded. (See Chapter 8.)

The challenge of this book is to increase the number of churches that develop social outreaches and to provide models of effective networking.

Volunteering and networking relationships should be developed during times when no emergency exists. This is vital to make volunteering more efficient and even possible in some cases, during times of disasters.

The time to repair the roof is when it's not raining!

Charitable organizations prior to the Great Depression most often had religious roots. It is still true today. Many national and secular voluntary organizations in the past century have been spearheaded by individuals motivated by their faith.

National service volunteer opportunities like the Peace Corps, VISTA (Volunteers in Service to America), and Senior Corps are well known and have been around for years.

BRIEF HISTORY OF NATIONAL COMMUNITY SERVICE PROGRAMS

In the 1930s, President Franklin D. Roosevelt established the Civilian Conservation Corps, which employed some three million men during the Great Depression days.

President John F. Kennedy created the Peace Corps in the early 1960s, and President Lyndon B. Johnson created Volunteers in Service to America (VISTA). Foster Grandparents, Senior Companions, and the Retired Senior Volunteer Program were initiated during the 1960s as well.

In the 1990s, President George H. W. Bush created the Commission on National and Community Service to administer grants to schools, higher education institutions, and community-based organizations.

CORPORATION FOR NATIONAL AND COMMUNITY SERVICES

In 1993, President Bill Clinton created the current Corporation for National and Community Service, combining the Commission on National Community Service with the federal domestic volunteer agency ACTION, uniting the full range of domestic service programs under one central organization.

The mission of the Corporation for National and Community Service is "to improve lives, strengthen communities, and foster civic engagement through service and volunteering."

Each year, the Corporation provides opportunities for approximately two million Americans of all ages and backgrounds to serve their communities and country through AmeriCorps, Senior Corps (Foster Grandparents, Senior Companion Program, and RSVP), and Learn and Serve America. Go to *www.cns.org* for more complete descriptions of these programs.

AMERICORPS

This is a national grant program that supports national service to meet critical needs in education, public safety, health, and the environment. This work is done through more than 2,100 non-profit organizations, public agencies, and faith-based organizations. Part of these efforts includes helping communities respond to disasters. More than 75,000 Americans participate in this program each year.

STATE SERVICE COMMISSIONS

Funding from the Corporation flows through governor-appointed State Service Commissions that determine funding priorities, make grants, mobilize volunteers, and promote community services in their states.

INVOLVEMENT IN DISASTERS
BY NONPROFITS AND CHURCHES

Until 1970, there was no coordination of nonprofit organizations responding to disasters. This resulted in haphazard assistance offered to disaster victims. There would often be duplication of services in some areas and total lack of services in others. There was also limited availability of training for volunteers. The mechanisms to coordinate communication and services between voluntary agencies were non-existent.

NATIONAL VOLUNTARY ORGANIZATIONS
ACTIVE IN DISASTERS

The need for coordination of these voluntary agencies was recognized during the 1960s, and various leaders of seven voluntary organizations met in Washington, D.C. on July 15, 1970 and formed what became known as the National Voluntary Organizations Active in Disasters. W. D. Dibrell of the American Red Cross is cited as the single most influential person in the formation of NVOAD.

The significant role of Christians and faith-based organizations in the formation of NVOAD is evidenced by the seven organizations involved with its formation. The seven organizations are:

- American Red Cross

- Salvation Army

- Christian Reformed World Relief Committee

- Mennonite Disaster Service

- National Catholic Disaster Relief Committee

- Society of St. Vincent de Paul

- Seventh Day Adventist

NVOAD has been an informal organization and was until recently totally run by volunteers from member organizations.

NVOAD PRINCIPLES

From its inception, the goal of NVOAD has been to network voluntary organizations involved with disasters to foster more effective service to victims. The slogan of NVOAD is: "Promoting Cooperation, Communication, Coordination and Collaboration during Disaster Preparedness, Response, Relief and Recovery."

GROWTH OF NVOAD

The organization has grown considerably since its inception, both in membership and in the significant role they have played in disaster relief efforts. As NVOAD has grown, it became necessary in 1976 to elect a nine-member Executive Committee to lead the organization. State VOADs have become a more significant part of NVOAD since the mid 1980s.

For further information about NVOAD organizations near you, go to: *www.nvoad.org/membersdb.php?members=State.*

It is of interest to note that the formation of the National Voluntary Organizations Active in Disasters (NVOAD) was actually organized several years before the formation of the Federal Emergency Management Agency (FEMA).

FORMATION OF FEDERAL EMERGENCY MANAGEMENT AGENCY

FEMA was formed in 1979 to consolidate several federal disaster and emergency agencies, including the Federal Insurance Administration, the U.S. Fire Administration, the Federal Disaster Assistance Administration, the Federal Preparedness Agency, and the Defense Civil Preparedness Agency.

NVOAD AND FEMA

NVOAD has worked closely with FEMA since FEMA was organized in 1979. Members of NVOAD are on the FEMA Advisory Board as well as the FEMA Board. This gives NVOAD the opportunity to represent concerns of voluntary agencies at the federal leadership level.

MANAGING SPONTANEOUS VOLUNTEERS

A major need that was identified during the response and recovery phases of 9-11 and the Katrina disasters was the need to incorporate volunteers who were not affiliated with any recognized organization.

Many of these unaffiliated volunteers had good intentions, resources, and needed skills, yet it was difficult to incorporate them into the disaster response activities. This resulted in many volunteers being underutilized and, in some cases, caused problems for professional emergency responders. This led to the realization that there needed to be better planning to incorporate unaffiliated volunteers.

This problem is being addressed through the National Voluntary Organizations Active in Disaster (NVOAD).

NATIONAL LEADERSHIP FORUM ON DISASTER VOLUNTEERISM

In response to this need, a National Leadership Forum on Disaster

Volunteerism was convened in April 2002. The Points of Light Foundation & Volunteer Center National Network, FEMA, and UPS led the forum. Participants from 45 different organizations from the volunteer and emergency management community developed recommendations and action steps to address the challenge of utilizing spontaneous, unaffiliated volunteers.

In early 2003, the National Voluntary Organizations Active in Disaster (NVOAD) established a Volunteer Management Committee to help develop additional tools and training to implement the recommendations that were made at the Forum. UPS funded a grant to support the work of this committee, which is staffed by the Points of Light Foundation.

The results of this effort have been the publication of the "Management of Unaffiliated Volunteers" and also "Concepts of Operation." Ten national principles have been published guiding the management of unaffiliated volunteers in times of emergency.

I will list all ten principles here and add a few comments. Those who plan to volunteer will benefit from understanding what is expected of them.

Principle #1: **Volunteering and Community Life**

Volunteering is a valuable part of every healthy community. Volunteers come from all segments of society and often provide essential services. Everyone has the potential to contribute strength and resources in times of emergency.

Principle #2: **The Value of Affiliation**

Ideally, all volunteers should be affiliated with an established organization and trained for specific disaster response activities. However, the spontaneous nature of individual volunteering is inevitable; therefore it must be anticipated, planned for, and managed.

I would like to insert here the fact that, in Chapter 8, I address how churches can form smaller networks. I recommend that each church network develop a liaison with recognized community volunteer networks (such as Community Organizations Active in Disasters (COADs) and Citizen Corps Councils so that in times of disaster there will not be any problem incorporating volunteers from the churches.

Several denominations have formed significant emergency volunteer structures within their organizations. The Southern Baptists are one of the leaders in this area.

Principle #3: **Volunteer Involvement in Four Phases**

There are valuable and appropriate roles for unaffiliated spontaneous volunteers in mitigation, preparedness, response, and recovery—as well as in other areas of community need. The response phase provides an opportunity to direct volunteers toward longer-term affiliation and community involvement.

Principle #4: **Management Systems**

Volunteers are a valuable resource when they are trained, assigned, and supervised within established emergency management systems. Similar to donations management, an essential element of every emergency management plan is the clear designation of responsibility for the on-site coordination of unaffiliated volunteers. The Volunteer Coordination Team (VCT) is the mechanism for ensuring the effective utilization of this human resource.

I want to add that you will be a greater asset to emergency efforts the more training you may receive in first aid and disaster preparedness through courses such as those offered by the Red Cross. Contact your local Red Cross or go to *www.redcross.org.*

Principle #5: **Shared Responsibility**

The mobilization, management, and support of volunteers are primarily a responsibility of local government and nonprofit sector agencies, with support from the state level. Specialized planning, information sharing, and a management structure are necessary to coordinate efforts and maximize the benefits of volunteer involvement.

Principle #6: **Volunteer Expectations**

Volunteers are successful participants in emergency management systems when they are flexible, self-sufficient, aware of risks, and willing to be coordinated by local emergency management experts. Volunteers must accept the obligation to "do no harm."

Principle #7: **The Impact on Volunteers**

The priority of volunteer activity is assistance to others. When this spontaneous activity is well managed, it also positively affects the volunteers themselves and thus contributes to the healing process of both individuals and the larger community.

Principle #8: **Build on Existing Capacity**

All communities include individuals and organizations that know how to mobilize and involve volunteers effectively. Emergency management experts and VOAD partners are encouraged to identify and utilize all existing capacity for integrating unaffiliated volunteers.

Principle #9: **Information Management**

Clear, consistent, and timely communication is essential to successful management of unaffiliated volunteers. A variety of opportunities and messages should be utilized in order to educate the public, minimize confusion, and clarify expectations.

Principle #10: **Consistent Terminology**

When referring to volunteer involvement in emergency management, it is helpful to use consistent terminology. The following terms and definitions are recommended:

> **Affiliated volunteers** are attached to a recognized voluntary or nonprofit organization and are trained for specific disaster response activities. Their relationship with the organization precedes the immediate disaster, and they are invited by that organization to become involved in a particular aspect of emergency management.

> **Unaffiliated volunteers** are not part of a recognized voluntary agency and often have no formal training in emergency response systems. They are not officially invited to become involved, but are motivated by a sudden desire to help others in times of trouble. They come with a variety of skills. They may come from within the affected area or from outside the area. (Also known as: "convergent," "emergent," "walk-in," or "spontaneous.")

(Again, this unaffiliated designation would normally apply to many within groups of church volunteers, but hopefully this problem will be mitigated by increased networking of the churches, which in turn develop relationships with recognized and affiliated voluntary emergency organizations.)

LOCAL VOLUNTEER CENTERS

To find local volunteer centers, use the following website: *www. pointsoflight.org/centers/find_center.cfm.* A major conclusion of the NVOAD Volunteer Management Committee is that it is imperative that many more citizens be integrated in the emergency management process due to limited resources available even combining federal, state, and local resources. **This includes pre-disaster planning!**

This will require greater levels of cooperation and partnering among the voluntary sector, professional first-responders, and all levels of government.

A major thrust of this book is to motivate readers to take responsibility for their own preparedness.

VOLUNTEER COORDINATION TEAMS

For those readers who desire to become actively involved with local disaster preparedness beyond your own personal preparedness, check with your local disaster response organizations. Many will have formed Volunteer Coordination Teams that have been integrated into local Emergency Operation Center organizational structures.

These VCTs will often include representatives from the local Community Emergency Response Team (CERT), Senior Corps (Foster Grandparents, Senior Companions, and RSVP programs), AmeriCorps/ VISTA, local churches, and other faith-based voluntary organizations.

For further information and to view examples of state plans that include Unaffiliated Volunteer Management, go to: *www.nemaweb.org/ donations_management/index.html.*

NATIONAL SERVICE PROGRAMS SINCE 9-11

The tragedy of September 11, 2001 led to the formation of many new national volunteer service programs under the umbrella of USA Freedom Corps. Many of these new programs are under the newly formed U.S. Department of Homeland Security and are designed to educate and empower Americans to take steps in preparation for and response to potential emergencies, both natural disasters and terrorist attacks.

USA FREEDOM CORPS

President George W. Bush created the USA Freedom Corps in 2002 to promote and expand the volunteer services in America by partnering with the national service programs, working to strengthen the non-profit sector, and helping connect individuals to volunteer opportunities. For a current list of partner volunteer organizations, go to *www.usafreedomcorps.gov.*

The USA Freedom Corps offers a Volunteer Network website, *www.volunteer.gov* or call 1-877-USA-CORPS to find existing volunteer service opportunities in your area. VolunteerMatch is an online service that matches volunteers with service opportunities in your community.

Since this book is on disaster preparedness, I will only emphasize a few of the new programs that were specifically formed to increase citizen participation in homeland security and disaster preparedness.

I encourage you to familiarize yourself with these programs and involve yourself in the areas in which you have personal interest. This will further equip you to be of service to your family, neighbors, community, and church networks.

CITIZEN CORPS

This is the president's new initiative, designed to engage volunteers in promoting safety in their communities. Citizen Corps activities are coordinated through the Department of Homeland Security. Citizen Corps asks each individual to take personal responsibility for being prepared and receiving training in first aid and emergency skills. Citizen Corps also challenges volunteers to support emergency responders, disaster relief, and community safety.

CITIZEN CORPS COUNCILS

Citizen Corps Councils have been formed in many communities. Currently, there are approximately 2,200 Citizen Corps Councils, which serve about three-fourths of the U.S. population.

Citizen Corps Councils help drive local citizen participation by coordinating Citizen Corps programs, developing community action plans, assessing possible threats, and identifying local resources for mitigation, response, and recovery. Go to *www.citizencorps.gov/councils/* for local voluntary organization information.

COMMUNITY EMERGENCY RESPONSE TEAM PROGRAM

The program Community Emergency Response Team (CERT) is administered under the Department of Homeland Security.

CERT educates people about disaster preparedness and trains them in basic disaster response skills, including fire safety, light search and rescue, and disaster medical operations.

Individuals trained through CERT can assist others in their neighborhood or workplace in case of emergencies. I highly recommend that you take advantage of this training if available in your area.

THE FIRE CORPS

The Fire Corps promotes the use of citizen advocates to increase the capacity of fire and rescue departments that are often in need of greater resources. Citizen advocates assist fire departments in areas such as teaching fire safety, youth programs, and administrative support.

Fire Corps is funded through the Department of Homeland Security and is managed and implemented through a partnership with the National Volunteer Fire Council, International Association of Fire Fighters, and the International Association of Fire Chiefs.

USAonWATCH-NEIGHBORHOOD WATCH

Neighborhood Watch programs have expanded beyond their traditional crime prevention role to help neighborhoods focus on disaster preparedness, emergency response, and terrorism awareness. Visit *www.USAonWATCH. org.* This program is administered by the National Sheriffs' Association and the Bureau of Justice Assistance, U.S. Department of Justice.

MEDICAL RESERVE CORPS PROGRAM

Medical, public health, and other individuals offer their expertise during local emergencies and other times of community need. These medical volunteers work in coordination with local emergency response teams and support public health initiatives such as prevention, immunization programs, blood drives, and other efforts. The Department of Health and Human Services administers this program.

VOLUNTEERS IN POLICE SERVICE

This program works to enhance the capacity of state and local law enforcement to utilize volunteers. VIPS is the gateway to resources and information about law enforcement volunteer programs. The VIPS program is funded by the Department of Justice and managed by the International Association of Chiefs of Police.

THE CITIZEN CORPS AFFILIATE PROGRAM

This program expands the resources and materials available to state and local communities by partnering with programs and organizations that offer resources for public education, outreach, and training or represent volunteers interested in making their communities safer or support emergency and disaster relief efforts.

Citizen Corps and the Corporation for National & Community Service work closely together to promote volunteer service activities that support homeland security and community safety.

FAITH-BASED COMMUNITY INVOLVEMENT IN DISASTERS

Our government has openly reached out to the faith-based community. Though there have been starts and stops and the laws have not been fully implemented, overall the efforts have been beneficial. It is important to remember that in our government are many committed believers.

Within the National Response Plan and the National Incident Management System, there are places for Christian NGOs and faith-based leadership to play significant roles in the coordination of relief efforts.

WHITE HOUSE FAITH-BASED AND COMMUNITY INITIATIVES

The White House Faith-Based and Community Initiatives brochure states: "Faith-based and community organizations (FBCOs) have a long tradition of helping Americans in need and together represent an integral part of our nation's social service network."

CHALLENGE TO THE FAITH-BASED COMMUNITY

This is the time for you and the entire faith-based community to rise to the challenge to play a more significant role in disaster preparedness and response.

What good is it, my brothers, if a man claims to have faith but has no deeds? Can such faith save him?

Suppose a brother or sister is without clothes and daily food.

If one of you says to him, "Go, I wish you well; keep warm and well fed," but does nothing about his physical needs, what good is it?

In the same way, faith by itself, if it is not accompanied by action, is dead.

But someone will say, "You have faith; I have deeds."

Show me your faith without deeds, and I will show you my faith by what I do.

—James 2:14-19

APPENDICES

APPENDIX A

HAZARD SPECIFIC PREPAREDNESS GUIDELINES

I am including in this appendix basic information on several of the more common hazards you may face. Some readers will not have Internet access; therefore, I have provided information on the following hazards: flooding, hurricanes, wildfires, thunderstorms, tornadoes, earthquakes, extreme heat, and winter storms.

DISASTERS THAT MAY REQUIRE EVACUATION

Evacuation measures are covered in Chapter 3 and emergency supplies for home, car, and workplace are covered in Chapter 4 and in Appendices C, F, G, and H. If evacuation is necessary, documents should be carried in a personal pouch around the waist (discussed in Chapter 6 and listed in Appendix I.) Chapter 7 covers pet care.

FLOODS

- If you are at risk for flooding, elevate your furnace, water heater, and electrical panel.

- Consider constructing barriers to stop floodwater from entering your home. Basement walls should be sealed with waterproofing compounds.

- Consider flood insurance. Refer to Chapter 6 and Appendix L.

- Make sure you have a full tank of gas.

How to Respond to Floods:

- Know the terms used for flooding hazards. A **flood watch** or **flash flood watch** means there is a possibility of flooding or flash flood in your area. *Be prepared to evacuate.*

- Keep informed by visiting NOAA Watch or local emergency

broadcasts. If the flooding hazard changes to **flood warning,** it means a flood is occurring and *you may be advised to evacuate immediately.* If the advisory indicates there is a **flash flood warning,** it means a flash flood is occurring and *you must seek higher ground immediately.*

- Do not walk through moving water, if at all possible. Even a small amount of water may knock you down.

- Do not drive into flooded areas. If you get caught by rising water, get out of your vehicle and move to higher ground.

- Stay away from downed power lines.

- Do not return to your home until authorities say it is safe. See Chapter 12 for more information on recovery post-flooding.

- Stay informed by listening to NOAA Weather Radio, watch TV, or stay tuned to the radio.

HURRICANES

- A **hurricane watch** means a hurricane is possible in your area. Be prepared to evacuate, if instructed by authorities.

- A **hurricane warning** is issued when a hurricane is expected in your area. Evacuate immediately when instructed to do so. If you or family members have special needs, be among the first to evacuate!

- Keep trees near home well trimmed.

- Have car filled with gas.

- Secure your property. Bring in all outdoor furniture and items that are not tied down. Cover windows with plywood or hurricane shutters.

- Follow your evacuation plans if told to do so.

- Be sure to let your out-of-state family know about your plans.

- If you are not able to evacuate for any reason, stay in an interior room that does not have windows, if possible. Remember, there may be a lull in the storm as the eye of the hurricane moves over. Stay in your home until told by authorities it is safe.

- Keep informed by listening to NOAA Weather Radio, watch TV, or stay tuned to the radio for weather alerts.

WILDFIRES

If you live in an area where you know you are at risk for wildfires, clear areas around your home of vegetation and plants that could easily catch fire. Go to the FEMA website or American Red Cross for more specific information. Do not return to your home until told by authorities it is safe.

THUNDERSTORMS AND LIGHTNING

- Remove dead tree branches or cut down rotting trees that might fall during a severe storm.

- Follow the 30/30 lightning safety rule. If you see lightning and hear thunder before you count to 30, you should go indoors and remain there for at least 30 minutes after the last clap of thunder.

- If the storm is severe, be sure to follow with the NOAA Weather Radio or other radio station for more weather information.

- Bring in or secure loose outdoor furniture.

- Do not use a corded phone except in an emergency. Cell phones and cordless phones are safe to use.

- Avoid use of computers and TVs during thunderstorms due to the possibility of power surges. Use surge protectors.

- Avoid showering or bathing during a thunderstorm.

- If you are caught outside when a storm hits, seek shelter in a building or automobile.

- If shelter is not available, go to the lowest area near you, but do not lie on the ground. Avoid hilltops and isolated trees in open fields.

- If you are out in a boat on open water, get to shore immediately and find shelter.

TORNADOES

- A **tornado watch** means a tornado is possible in your area. Listen to your NOAA Weather Radio, local radio or TV news.

- A **tornado warning** means a tornado is actually occurring and you need to take shelter immediately.

- Go to the area in your home where you have pre-determined is the safest place.

    o Storm cellar or basement is safest.

    o If underground area is not available, go to an interior hallway or interior room on the lowest floor possible. Go to the center of the room and stay away from windows, doors and outside walls.

    o Remain in the sheltered area until the danger has passed.

- If you are caught in your vehicle or in a trailer or mobile home, plan to go to a building with a strong foundation if at all possible.

- If you cannot get to a safe shelter, lie flat in a ditch or low-lying area. Do not get under an overpass or bridge.

- After a tornado, do not enter damaged buildings. Watch out for downed power lines and any gas leaks.

- Help injured or trapped people.

- Stay informed regarding the weather conditions and any other emergency broadcast information.

EARTHQUAKES

- Securely fasten shelves to walls.

- Store heavier and larger items on lower shelves or in cabinets with latches.

- Inspect electrical wiring and gas connections and repair, if needed.

- Secure water heater to wall studs with straps and bolt to the floor.

- Store any flammable or toxic materials in cabinets with doors and latches.

- Pre-identify safe places in your home or office should an earthquake occur. Getting under heavy furniture is the best protection from falling debris.

- Stay away from windows, mirrors, and other glass.

- Avoid exterior walls, exits, and areas directly outside of a building, where you are at greater risk from falling debris.

- Be sure you know how to turn off your electricity and gas, if needed. Check for gas leaks after an earthquake. If you suspect there is a leak, leave immediately and notify the gas company. If possible, turn off the gas outside at the main valve.

- Expect aftershocks for several hours or even days after the initial earthquake.

EXTREME HEAT

- Make sure your home cooling system is working properly.

- Make sure your home is well insulated and the weather stripping around doors and windows is in place and in good repair.

- Avoid being outdoors during the hottest time of the day.

- Avoid strenuous outdoor activities such as yard work, sports, etc.

- Learn about heat exhaustion and heat stroke.

- Maintain your hydration by drinking plenty of water. Avoid alcoholic beverages.

- Eat light, nutritious meals.

- When outdoors, wear loose-fitting clothing and a hat.

- Never leave children or pets alone in closed vehicles.

- Keep informed about weather conditions.

WINTER STORMS AND EXTREME COLD

- Make sure your home is well insulated and the weather stripping around doors and windows is in place and in good repair.

- Have plenty of firewood available if you have a fireplace.

- Become familiar with the winter weather terms:

    o **Freezing rain** creates a coat of ice on roads, walkways, and can destroy trees and vegetation.

    o **Sleet** is rain that turns to pellets of ice. Roads freeze and become very slippery.

    o **Winter Weather Advisory** means that cold, ice, and snow are expected.

    o **Winter Storm Watch** means that severe weather is possible within the next 24-48 hours.

o **Winter Storm Warning** indicates that severe winter conditions have started or will begin soon.

o **Blizzard Warning** means heavy snow and strong winds will produce a blinding snow, poor visibility, deep snow drifts, and life-threatening wind chill.

o **Frost/Freeze Warning** indicates that temperatures below freezing are expected.

If you have been advised to expect a winter storm or extreme cold, take the following steps:

- Make sure your emergency supplies kit for home, car and personal emergency kit are updated. Be sure adequate clothing and blankets and sleeping bags are part of the preparation.

- Make sure you have adequate food and water supplies for the whole family for a minimum of 3 days, though I recommend at least 2 weeks' supply.

- Make sure your vehicle is full of gas.

- Stay informed regarding the weather conditions and any other emergency broadcast information.

The specific hazards covered at the FEMA website, *http://www.ready. gov/america/beinformed/index.html,* can be accessed and downloaded to your computer. I recommend that you go to the site and print out all hazard preparations you anticipate you might face.

The hazards covered are:

- Biological Threat
www.ready.gov/america/beinformed/biological.html

- Chemical Threat
www.ready.gov/america/beinformed/chemical.html

- Earthquakes
www.ready.gov/america/beinformed/earthquakes.html

- Explosions
www.ready.gov/america/beinformed/explosions.html

- Extreme Heat
www.ready.gov/america/beinformed/heat.html

- Fires
www.ready.gov/america/beinformed/fires.html
(Also refer to Chapter 4.)

- Floods
www.ready.gov/america/beinformed/floods.html

- Hurricanes
www.ready.gov/america/beinformed/hurricanes.html

- Influenza Pandemic
www.ready.gov/america/beinformed/influenza.html

- Landslide and Debris Flow (Mudslide)
www.ready.gov/america/beinformed/landslides.html

- Nuclear Threat
www.ready.gov/america/beinformed/nuclear.html

- Radiation Threat
www.ready.gov/america/beinformed/radiation.html

- Thunderstorms
www.ready.gov/america/beinformed/thunderstorms.html

- Tornadoes
www.ready.gov/america/beinformed/tornadoes.html

- Tsunamis
www.ready.gov/america/beinformed/tsunamis.html

- Volcanoes
www.ready.gov/america/beinformed/volcanoes.html

- Wildfires
www.ready.gov/america/beinformed/wildfires.html

- Winter Storms and Extreme Cold
www.ready.gov/america/beinformed/winter.html

- State and Local Information
www.ready.gov/america/local/index.html

Another excellent FEMA website for hazard specific information is: *http://www.fema.gov/hazard/.*

APPENDIX B

FOOD ITEMS, STORAGE, AND COOKING RECOMMENDATIONS

EMERGENCY FOOD SUPPLY CHOICES

For your emergency food supply, choose foods that do not require refrigeration or special preparation. Select foods that require very little water or cooking. Avoid foods that will make you thirsty.

To decide how much food to store, calculate the amount of food you need for two meals per person per day for 2 weeks. The easiest way to do this is to plan a daily menu to help you estimate quantities of food to store. The government only recommends having a 3-day food supply, but that is not realistic for major disasters.

STORE WHAT YOU EAT, EAT WHAT YOU STORE

As I indicated earlier in Chapter 4, some people recommend 3-6 months of food storage. This gets to be very expensive for many families. Following the "store what you eat, and eat what you store" principle will allow you to achieve this goal without breaking your monthly budget.

If some of the foods you choose to store are not normally part of your diet, begin to occasionally use these items and learn to prepare them so this preparation becomes routine for you.

- Whole grains: wheat, barley, white or yellow corn, oats, rice. (Consider buying a grain mill.)

- If you are allergic to wheat and wheat products, consider spelt, which is used in cooking and baking just as you would wheat.

- Dried grains

- Dried fruit

- Beans (black beans, black-eyed peas, chickpeas, kidney beans, lentils, lima beans, navy beans, soybeans, split peas, white beans, pinto beans, peanuts, etc.) Beans are very nutritious and can be cooked whole, ground into flour, or sprouted.

- Nuts, including canned nuts (almonds, black walnuts, brazil nuts, cashews, filberts, pistachios, pecans, peanuts)

- Seeds (alfalfa, flax, pumpkin, radish, sesame and sun flower—non-salted)

- Canned foods low in sodium with high liquid content

- Powdered milk (boxed)

- Dried eggs

- Dehydrated foods (Learn how to dehydrate your own vegetables, fruit and meats.)

- MREs (Meals Ready to Eat), available in wilderness and sporting good stores

- Canning your own fruits and vegetables (Canning is a lost art today, but there are books available.)

- Freeze-dried foods (The drawback is that water and cooking are required.)

- Peanut butter

- Low-sodium crackers, granola bars

- Trail mix

- Instant coffee, tea

- Sweeteners: corn syrup, brown sugar, honey, maple syrup, molasses, sorghum

- Salt and other spices

- Baking powder, baking soda, yeast, cooking oils

- **Do not forget a manual can opener!**

TIPS ON BULK FOOD STORAGE

If you are storing in bulk, 20 pounds of wheat or other grains will feed one person for one month; 80 pounds will feed a family of four for one month. Ten pounds of beans will feed one person for one month; 40 pounds will feed a family of four for one month). Twenty pounds of powdered milk will feed one person for one month; 80 pounds will feed a family of four for one month. Three quarts of oil are needed per month per person.

FOOD STORAGE CONTAINERS

Unless the food you buy is already packaged in a long-term storage package, transfer food into food-grade plastic containers or metal containers with air-tight seals to protect from insects and rodents.

Once a bucket or can is opened, be prepared to reseal it. "Gamma Seal" lids work well and allow access to 5- and 6-gallon plastic containers. Reusable plastic lids are made for No. 10 cans. Refer to *Don't Get Caught with Your Pantry Down,* by James Talmage Stevens to source different types of lids.

Store food away from gasoline or other fuels, especially if in plastic containers. Plastic containers may allow odors to penetrate and affect the contents. Also, do not set plastic containers directly on concrete because plastic will absorb moisture.

Remember to:

- Store food in cool, dry area.

- Rotate emergency food stocks every 6 to 12 months. (Some items can be stored indefinitely.)

- Include special dietary needs.

- Do consider planting a small garden and/or have garden seeds for vegetables and other foods.

- Do not discuss information about your emergency food and water supply outside of your family.

SAFETY AND SANITATION DOS AND DON'TS

Do:

- Keep garbage in closed containers and dispose outside, burying garbage, if necessary.

- Discard any food that has come into contact with contaminated flood water.

- Use only pre-prepared canned baby formula for infants or powdered formula with treated water.

- Discard any food that has an unusual odor, color, or texture.

Don't:

- Don't eat foods from cans that are swollen, dented, or corroded, even though the product may look safe.

- Don't eat any food that has been at room temperature for two hours. Note: Thawed food can usually be eaten if it is still "refrigerator cold." It can be re-frozen if it still contains ice crystals. To be safe, remember, "When in doubt, throw it out."

ALTERNATIVE COOKING SOURCES

Alternative cooking sources in times of emergency include candle warmers and fondue pots. Charcoal grills and camp stoves are for outdoor use only.

Campfire or fireplace cooking is sometimes referred to as "Dutch-oven cooking." If interested in learning more about this technique, go to *http://www.dutchovencookware.com*

Solar cooking is also an option. Go to *www.solarcookers.org* and *solarcookers.org/plans* to explore this topic.

CANNED FOODS

Commercially canned food may be eaten out of the can without warming.

If you desire to heat the food in the can, be sure the can is thoroughly washed and cleaned first with a disinfectant. Remove any labels from the can and then open the can before heating.

KEEPING FOOD SAFE
WITHOUT ELECTRICAL POWER

- Look for alternate storage space for your perishable food. (We had to move our frozen foods to a neighbor's home when we lost power for 4 days.)

- Twenty pounds of dry ice can keep a 10-cubic-foot freezer below freezing for 3-4 days. Handle dry ice carefully with dry gloves to protect your skin.

APPENDIX C

CHECKLIST HOME EMERGENCY SUPPLIES KIT
(SEE CHAPTER 4.)

Essential food (Appendix B)   _____

Special dietary foods (if needed)   _____

Water (1 gal./person/day; minimum 3 days   _____
(14-day supply is recommended.)

Portable water filtration system   _____

Water purification tablets or solution   _____

Portable, battery-powered radio or TV   _____
with extra batteries or hand-rechargeable radio

Flashlights and extra batteries   _____
(or flashlights that don't require batteries
 or solar-powered lights)

First aid kit and manual   _____
(See chapter 7 and Appendix D.)

Insect repellent (mosquito netting)   _____

Smoke hoods (especially if living in high-rise   _____
or multi-storied buildings)

Crowbar (small)   _____

Roll of duct tape (flattened)   _____

Nylon cord (550-lb. test)   _____

Sanitation and hygiene items   _____

Waterproof matches or matches in a waterproof container _____

Lighters _____

Heavy-duty plastic garbage bags _____

Kitchen accessories and cooking utensils including a manual can opener (Camping cookware may work well.) _____

Whistle _____

Signal flare _____

Small tool kit (wrench, pliers, other tools) Or use a multi-tool (e.g., Kershaw locking pliers or Leatherman Crunch.) _____

Scissors (preferably EMT scissors, also called bandage scissors) _____

Needle and thread (sewing kit) _____

Extra set of house keys and car keys _____

Plastic sheeting _____

Medium-sized plastic bucket with tight lid _____

Disinfectant and household chlorine bleach _____

Small shovel _____

Small canister, ABC-type fire extinguisher _____

Tube tent _____

Compass _____

Work gloves   _____

Extra clothing   _____
(Recommended clothing will vary according
to where you live and weather you anticipate
facing if evacuation is required.)

Rain gear   _____

Prescription medications   _____
(Be sure to rotate regularly so as not to allow the
medications to become outdated.)

Eye glasses, contact lens solutions   _____
(Be sure to renew regularly.)

Goggles for emergency eye protection   _____
(Can use simple swimming goggles.)

Hearing aid batteries (if applicable)   _____

Items for infants (formula, diapers, bottles, _____
pacifiers, etc.)
(Make sure that formula is renewed regularly.)

Emergency contact list and phone numbers _____
(Include police, fire, doctor, hospital, schools,
electric, gas, water companies; place list next to
phone in the home as well as in emergency Grab-
and-Go bag.)

Family emergency contact list and phone _____
numbers
(Include out-of-area family and E-mail
addresses in case Internet access should
become available. Put in waterproof
container. Include pictures of each family member.)

Map of local area and or places you might _____
plan to go to if evacuating (in waterproof container)

Photocopies of credit and identification cards.   _____
(Be sure to place in plastic or waterproof container.)

Copies of important documents such as insurance   _____
and vital records in waterproof container
(See Appendix E for more complete list.)

Cash and some coins (water-tight container)   _____
(It is recommended that you have at least $500 in
small bills; some suggest up to $3,000. You
cannot be guaranteed access to ATMs or bank
accounts, and small bills will make it easier if
paying for services or goods.)

Paper, pens, pencils (waterproof container)   _____
(Waterproof notebooks may be found at sporting
goods stores.)

**For those living in a cold climate, add the following items to your
emergency supplies kit:**

Jacket/coat/the least bulky that provides   _____
adequate warmth

Long pants, long-sleeved shirt   _____

Sturdy shoes like hiking boots   _____

Hat/head covering/gloves/scarf   _____

Sleeping bag or blanket (per person)   _____

Additional Items for Consideration:

Emergency transportation   _____
(bicycle, moped)

Self-defense equipment   _____

Gas masks   _____

Fire escape ladder   _____

Inflatable raft   _____

Portable stove   _____

Stove fuel   _____

Kitty litter for sanitation purposes   _____

Chlorophyll to reduce fecal odor   _____

Safety helmet   _____

APPENDIX D

FIRST AID KIT
(SEE CHAPTER 7.)

Two good publications to back up your knowledge of first aid are the Red Cross first aid manual (available at Red Cross) and *Where There Is No Doctor, A Village Health Care Handbook,* by David Werner with Carol Thuman and Jane Maxwell, updated in 2007. Go to *http://www.hesperian. org/index.php* to obtain a copy. The Hesperian organization also publishes a book entitled *Where There Is No Dentist.*

First Aid Kit:

Band-Aids (many assorted sizes)   _____

Antiseptic/alcohol wipes   _____

Hand sanitizer bottles (2)   _____

Topical antibiotic ointment   _____

Topical hydrocortisone cream   _____

Hydrogen peroxide   _____

Tube of petroleum jelly   _____

Sunscreen   _____

Thermometer   _____

Lighter   _____

Several pairs of latex gloves   _____

Sterile gauze pads, 2-inch (10)   _____

Sterile gauze pads, 4-inch (10)   _____

Sterile roller bandages, 2-inch (5)   _____

Sterile roller bandages, 4-inch (5)   _____

Sterile cotton balls (small pack)   _____

Adhesive bandage tape, hypoallergenic: 1-inch   _____

Triangular bandages (3)   _____

Bandage scissors (EMT scissors)   _____

Maxi sanitary napkins (5) for blood absorption   _____
from major wounds

Irrigating syringe   _____

Ace bandages, 2-inch, 3-inch and 4-inch   _____
(2 each size)

Two tweezers (one regular size, one small)   _____

Needle   _____
(If you have professional training, consider
including suture material and set.)

Scalpel with extra blades   _____

Pain relievers (non-aspirin pain relievers such   _____
as acetaminophen, ibuprofen, etc.)
(Use whatever you are familiar with.)

Bismuth subsalicylate (Pepto-Bismol)   _____
(Check with your doctor for children's dosages.)

Antacids   _____

Stool softeners   _____

Antifungal ointment/cream (e.g. miconazole)   _____

Visine eye drops   _____

Cough and cold medications (OTC)   _____

Diphenhyramine (Benadryl)   _____
(This is an antihistamine used for hives,
allergic rhinitis, etc. Check with your doctor
for children's dosages.)

If you or a family member is severely allergic   _____
to insect bites, or foods, you may need a doctor's
Rx for Epi-Pen; learn more at *www.epipen.com.*

Poison ingestion Rx:

Syrup of ipecac   _____
(Use only if advised by a poison control center.)

Activated charcoal   _____
(Use if advised by a poison control center.)

PRESCRIPTION MEDICATIONS FOR FAMILY MEMBERS

Antibiotics obtained through doctor's Rx   _____

Current prescription meds for family   _____

Ophthalmic antibiotic (through doctor's Rx)   _____

Injectable atropine (requires training)   _____
(Used against Zebra: poison gas terrorism.
See *www.fema.gov* for further preparations
for such terrorist acts.)

OTHER CONSIDERATIONS

Contact lenses, extra pair   _____

Contact lens solutions required   _____

APPENDIX E

VITAL RECORDS AND DOCUMENTS

All essential documents should be carried in lightweight, water-resistant containers. One source for such containers can be found at the website *www.docukeeper.com*. It is recommended that the document container be stored in a fire-resistant, waterproof safe or lock box. Have it readily available to put in your Grab-and-Go bag.

Refer to **Appendix I** where I recommend you place some of these items in a pouch around your waist and not in your grab-and-go bag. Keep the pouch documents in a separate waterproof container.

Have copies of the essential documents already in your grab-and-go bag just in case you do not have time to transfer the originals from your safe/lock box.

Consider having copies (or originals in some cases) of all essential documents stored away from your home such as in a bank safe deposit box. Make sure other family members that need to know are aware of this storage site and that appropriate individuals are authorized to have access to them, if needed.

Some of your legal documents (copies or originals) may already be stored at a law office. Asking other family members or close friends to keep copies of certain documents may be another option for you. I kept copies of important documents for my parents before they passed away.

INTERNET "SAFE DEPOSIT BOX"

Another excellent way to store important documents is to make digital copies and store them a remote site on the Internet. There are companies that provide these services, but if you do not want this expense, you can scan your own documents and store them on the Internet. You may also make copies on other storage disks and keep the copies in several places (at least one being a remote site). There is the risk of loss of data due to technological reasons or even sabotage, but this risk is minimized if you have more than one copy.

PERSONAL IDENTIFICATION DOCUMENTS

- **Driver's license** original in wallet/purse or photo ID card   _____

  Copy stored in safe/lockbox   _____

  Copy in Grab-and-Go bag   _____

- **Passport original** (or naturalization papers)   _____

  Copy stored in safe/lockbox   _____

  Copy in Grab-and-Go bag   _____

  and office emergency kit   _____

- **Social Security card** original in wallet/purs   _____

  Copy in safe/lockbox if you carry original   _____

  Copy in Grab-and-Go bag   _____

- **Birth certificate** (certified with original seal)   _____

  (I recommend you have more than one certified copy in an off-site location.)   _____

  Copy in Grab-and-Go bag   _____

MEDICAL RECORDS

- **Personal medical records** in safe/lockbox   _____

  Include immunization records.   _____

  Copies in Grab-and-Go Bag   _____

INSURANCE POLICIES

- **Life insurance** original in safe/lockbox   _____

  Copy in Grab-and-Go bag   _____

- **Home owners/renters insurance** in safe/lockbox   _____

  Flood insurance, if needed   _____

  Earthquake insurance, if needed   _____

  Copies in Grab-and-Go bag   _____

- **Health insurance policy**   _____

  Policy ID card in wallet/purse

  Copy in Grab-and-Go bag   _____

- **Disability insurance policy** in safe/lockbox   _____

  Copy in Grab-and-Go bag   _____

- **Auto/vehicular insurance policy** (policies)   _____

  Copies in Grab-and-Go bag   _____

  Copies in vehicles   _____

DOCUMENTATION OF INVESTMENTS/TRUSTS

- **Stock/bond certificates** in safe/lockbox   _____

  Copies in Grab-and-Go bag   _____

- **Trust documents** in safe/lockbox   _____

  Copies in Grab-and-Go bag   _____

DOCUMENTATION OF DEBTS

Maintaining good credit during times of disaster and not incurring penalties or late fees is important. Even if creditors are lenient with you, it will save you much time and effort if you are able to maintain normal payments during emergency situations. For this, you need proper documentation.

- **Loan papers** to be stored in safe/lockbox   _____

     Mortgage (most recent statement)   _____

     Other real estate   _____

     Auto loan papers / monthly statement   _____

     Other vehicular loans   _____

     Copies in Grab-and-Go bag   _____

- **Deeds and titles** to real estate in safe/lockbox   _____

     Copies in Grab-and-Go bag   _____

- **Titles to vehicles**; registrations in safe/lockbox   _____

     Copies in Grab-and-Go bag   _____

- **Credit cards**- copies of both sides in safe/lockbox   _____

     Copies of most recent statement (updated)   _____

     Copies in Grab-and-Go bag   _____

DOCUMENTS IN BANK SAFE DEPOSIT BOX

- **Wills**   _____

- **Living wills**   _____

- **Power-of-attorney** (original) _____

- **Marriage certificate** (or divorce decree) _____

You may decide to keep other major documents in your bank safe deposit box rather than the safe/lockbox at home. It is a good idea to give a copy of your will/ living will or trust to the individual or layer or institution that is designated as the executor.

Be sure to keep an extra key for the deposit box in your Grab-and-Go bag.

SAFEGUARD YOUR BUSINESS RECORDS

Backing up client contact information, payroll records, accounts receivable, and accounts payable are the most essential pieces of information you will need for a quick start-up of your business following a disaster.

The Internet "Safe Deposit Box" option would be a particularly good option for a business. Also, keep several full backup copies of all financial data and store one in a remote place more than 50 miles from your location.

Many businesses do full backup of data daily and use different media for each day so that, in fact, they have at least five backup disks at any one time. Sending the backup data digitally to a remote site is the easiest way to do it daily.

If your business has real estate debts, vehicular loans, or credit card debt, follow the guidelines given above for personal debt documentation and storage.

WORD OF CAUTION ABOUT IDENTITY THEFT

During times of emergencies and disasters, if you have to evacuate or leave your home in a hurry and/or you experience significant damage to your home and property, you will be more vulnerable to identity theft. Guard carefully all the documentation you carry with you in your Grab-and-Go bag and in your wallet, purse, or waist pouch.

APPENDIX F

CAR EMERGENCY SUPPLIES LIST

CHECKLIST CAR EMERGENCY SUPPLIES

Jumper cables   _____

Flares   _____

Flat tire inflation canister (non-explosive)   _____

Spare tire and jack   _____

First aid supplies   _____

Water, several gallons
(Frequently replenish supply.)   _____

High energy foods/power bars   _____

Small tool kit   _____

Flashlight and batteries or flashlight
that does not need batteries   _____

Small shovel, foldable   _____

Road maps
(Consider hand-held GPS device if your car
does not have a GPS.)   _____

Blankets   _____

Fire extinguisher, small (ABC type)   _____

Antifreeze, can of oil   _____

Backpack to store car emergency supplies   _____

Seasonal supplies, such as umbrellas, rain gear,   _____
ice scraper

     Several disaster preparedness manuals have a more extensive list of recommended items for the car emergency supplies.

ADDITIONAL ITEMS TO CONSIDER

Towing line or chain   _____

Sanitation items: bed pan, towelettes,   _____
kitty litter, small trash bags

Emergency battery charger   _____

Photovoltaic trickle battery charger   _____

Extra pair of shoes, gloves   _____

Toiletries, soap, etc.   _____

Cell phone charger left in car at all times   _____

Battery-powered radio   _____

Sleeping bag(s), particularly if winter storms   _____
are possible

APPENDIX G
WORKPLACE EMERGENCY SUPPLIES KIT
(See Chapter 4.)

WORKPLACE EMERGENCY SUPPLIES KIT

Personal first aid kit   _____

Prescription medications
(Rotate monthly.)   _____

Comfortable walking shoes or boots
for emergencies   _____

Emergency food and water   _____

Flashlight (type that does not require batteries)   _____

Small emergency radio   _____

Mini-pry bar   _____

Smoke hood, in case of fire   _____

Extra keys (home and vehicles)   _____

Duct tape   _____

Nylon cord (550-lb. test, if you work in multi-
story building)   _____

Rain gear, umbrella   _____

Copies of ID, driver's license, passport, etc.   _____

Readily accessible Grab-and-Go bag contains
emergency workplace supplies.   _____

APPENDIX H

PERSONAL EMERGENCY SUPPLIES KIT

BARE BONES PERSONAL EMERGENCY KIT

Flashlight, small, waterproof   _____

Whistle   _____

First aid kit, small   _____

Water purification tablets   _____

Smoke hood or partial face respirator,   _____
especially if you live in a high-rise or use subways

Cord (550-lb. test, monofilament fishing line,   _____
minimum 30 feet)

ADDITIONAL BASIC PERSONAL
EMERGENCY KIT ITEMS

If airports and restricted public buildings are not an issue, the following basic personal emergency kit items are recommended in addition to those listed above:

Multi-tool (e.g., Leatherman locking pliers)   _____

Mini-pry bar   _____

Weatherproof matches   _____

EMT shears (bandage scissors)   _____

Food, high-energy bars   _____

Extra money   _____

Good walking shoes (wear or have available)   _____

APPENDIX I

PERSONAL POUCH DOCUMENTS
(See Chapter 6.)

When evacuation becomes necessary and you must leave your home, put your Grab-and-Go bag in your car. I recommend you also put the essential identification documents in a special pouch to be carried on your person at all times. This greatly reduces the risk of loss or theft of these vital documents. Refer to Chapter 6.

LIST OF POUCH DOCUMENTS AND OTHER ITEMS

Passport   _____

Driver's license   _____

Social Security card(s) for self, family   _____

Bank cards and/or credit cards   _____

Money (most in the pouch, some in your pocket)   _____

List of immunizations with dates   _____

Medical alert information (or wear tag or wristband)   _____

List of critical family contact numbers   _____

List of emergency numbers (police, fire hospitals, doctor, etc).   _____

Extra set of car and house keys   _____

Prepaid phone cards   _____

APPENDIX J

FAMILY COMMUNICATIONS PLAN AND CHECKLIST

Contact card is completed for each family member. _____

This information has been sent to each child's school. _____

Medical release form filled out and sent to school
to have on file in case of emergencies. _____

Each family member has a prepaid phone card. _____

Family members carry pictures of each
family member with clearly defined features. _____

This family communication information has been
shared with out-of-area family members. _____

Family safety notification plan is in place. _____

Friends and "need-to-know" individuals have
all been notified of this plan _____

CONTACT INFORMATION FOR EACH FAMILY MEMBER

Contact name: _____

Telephone (home): _____

Telephone (cell): _____

E-mail address: _____

Out-of-state contact name: _____

Telephone (home): _____

Telephone (cell): _____

E-mail address: _____

Neighborhood meeting place: _____

Meeting place telephone: _____

Dial 911 in emergencies (placed on each card).

Additional important phone numbers and information:

_____

_____

_____

I have made hard copies of the family   _____
communication plan and put in waterproof
containers as part of my emergency kits.

Family member meeting place(s) identified   _____
in case of a major national catastrophe.

Go to *www.ready.gov* to download family communication forms, or you
may create your own. Be sure to laminate the cards to make them more
durable. These cards should be carried by each family member at all
times.

APPENDIX K

GLOSSARY OF TERMS AND AGENCIES

Citizen Corps: A new president's initiative, designed to engage volunteers in promoting safety in their communities. Citizen Corps activities are coordinated through the Department of Homeland Security. Citizen Corps asks each individual to take personal responsibility to be prepared and to get training in first aid and emergency skills. Citizen Corps also challenges volunteers to support emergency responders, disaster relief and community safety.

Citizen Corps Councils: Help drive local citizen participation by coordinating Citizen Corps programs, developing community action plans, assessing possible threats and identifying local resources for mitigation, response and recovery from emergencies and disasters.

CERT: Community Emergency Response Team
This program is administered under the Department of Homeland Security. CERT educates people about disaster preparedness and trains them in basic disaster response skills, including fire safety, light search and rescue, and disaster medical operations.

COAD: Community Organizations Active in Disasters

DHS: Department of Homeland Security

EAS: The Emergency Alert System; can address the entire nation on very short notice in case of national emergencies.

EOC: Emergency Operations Center
State, county, and local EOCs are the physical location at which the coordination of information and resources to support incident management activities normally take place. EOCs are usually organized by major functional services (fire, law enforcement, medical services, etc.) or by jurisdiction (city, county, region, etc.) or a combination of the two.

ERT-A: Emergency Response Team-Advance
When an incident occurs, the RRCC deploys a DHS/FEMA-led Emergency Response Team—Advance Element (ERT-A), including rapid needs assessment personnel to state operating facilities and incident sites to assess the situation and gauge federal support requirements and make preliminary arrangements to set up federal field facilities.

ERT-N: National Emergency Response Team
If the incident overextends regional resources or the event poses potentially significant consequences, DHS Headquarters may deploy a National Emergency Response Team (ERT-N) to coordinate the initial response.

ESF: Emergency Support Function
(ESFs) are the primary means through which the federal government provides assistance to state, local, and tribal governments or to federal department and agencies conducting missions of primary federal responsibility.

FEMA: Federal Emergency Management Agency

FIRST: Federal Incident Response Support Team
Depending on the nature of an incident, a Federal Incident Response Support Team (FIRST) may be deployed to the scene to support state operations. FIRST provides technical assistance to assess the situation, identify critical and unmet needs, provide protective action recommendations, and establish incident support facilities. The FIRST coordinates with the ERT-A and integrates into the Joint Field Office when established.

IC and ICP: Incident Commander and Incident Command Post
When an incident occurs, the appropriate jurisdictional authority (federal, state, or local) designates a single Incident Commander with overall incident management responsibility. Most jurisdictions pre-designate their Incident Commander in preparedness plans. The Incident Commander directs the operations of the Incident Command Post (ICP), which is usually located at or in the immediate vicinity of the incident site.

The ICP is the tactical level, on-scene incident command and management organization location. The ICP is comprised of designated management officials and responders from federal, state, local, and tribal agencies, as well as private-sector and non-governmental organizations (NGOs).

INS: Incident of National Significance
Is an actual or potential high-impact event that requires major coordination of the federal response in order to save lives, minimize damage, and provide the basis for long-term community and economic recovery.

JFO: Joint Field Office
When an incident occurs, a *temporary* federal facility, called a Joint Field Office (JFO), is established locally.

NGOs: Non-Governmental Organizations

NIMS: National Incident Management System

NIPP and CIPAC: National Infrastructure Protection Plan and Critical Infrastructure Protection Advisory Committee
The NRP recognizes the private sector as a key partner in domestic incident management. For coordination with the owners and operators of the nation's critical infrastructure, the Department of Homeland Security and federal agencies utilize mechanisms established under the National Infrastructure Protection Plan (NIPP), including the Critical Infrastructure Protection Advisory Committee (CIPAC).

NOAA and NWR: National Oceanic & Atmospheric Administration Weather Radio:
Is a nationwide network of radio stations broadcasting continuous information directly from a nearby National Weather Service office to specially configured NOAA weather radio receivers.

NOC: The National Operations Center is comprised of five sub-elements:

NOC-Interagency Watch is a standing 24/7 interagency organization that fuses law enforcement, national intelligence, emergency response, and private sector reporting.

NOC-Watch: The NOC-Watch facilitates homeland security information-sharing and operational coordination with other federal, state, local, tribal and non-governmental emergency operation centers.

NOC-NRCC: National Response Coordination Center, which monitors potential or developing incidents and supports efforts of regional and field components.

NOC-I&A: Intelligence and Analysis is responsible for interagency intelligence collection requirements, analysis, production, and product dissemination for the Department of Homeland Security.

NOC-BICC: National Infrastructure Coordination Center monitors the nation's critical infrastructure and key resources on an ongoing basis.

NOC-Planning: Interagency Planning Element
conducts strategic level operational incident management planning and coordination.

NRP: **The National Response Plan**

NRP Headquarters is composed of five major elements:

    IAC: Incident Advisory Council

    DRG: Domestic Readiness Group

    NOC: National Operations Center

    SIOC: Strategic Information Operations Center

    PFO: Principal Federal Officer

NVOAD: National Voluntary Organizations Active in Disaster
The need for coordination of these voluntary agencies was recognized during the 1960s and various leaders of seven voluntary organizations met in Washington, D.C. on July 15, 1970 and formed what became known as the National Voluntary

Organizations Active in Disaster.

RRCC: Regional Response Coordination Centers
The Department of Homeland Security through FEMA (DHS/ FEMA) has regional offices that coordinate regional responses to disasters. The Regional Response Coordination Centers (RRCC) are standing facilities.

SSC: State Service Commission
Funding from the Corporation flows through governor-appointed State Service Commissions that determine funding priorities, make grants, mobilize volunteers, and promote community services in their states.

Unified Command:
Is an application of the NIMS/Incident Command System (ICS) used when there is more than one agency with jurisdiction over a particular incident or when incidents cross political jurisdictions.

VCT: Volunteer Coordination Team
Volunteers are a valuable resource when they are trained, assigned, and supervised within established emergency management systems. The Volunteer Coordination Team (VCT) is the mechanism for ensuring the effective utilization of volunteers.

These Volunteer Coordination Teams will often include representatives from the local Community Emergency Response Team (CERT), Retired Senior Volunteer Program (RSVP), AmeriCorps/VISTA, local churches, and other faith-based voluntary organizations.

To find local volunteer centers, use the following website: *www.pointsoflight.org/center/find_centers.cfm.*

APPENDIX L

EMERGENCY RESOURCES FOLLOWING DISASTERS

Many agencies provide direct assistance following a disaster. If your church has developed a compassionate ministry program, this would be an excellent place to start.

Two major emergency disaster follow-up resources are:

Salvation Army: *http://www.salvationarmy.org*

American Red Cross: *www.redcross.org*

FEDERAL ASSISTANCE PROGRAMS

The federal government works in cooperation with state authorities and private firms; together, they offer a wide range of disaster insurance, loan and grant programs.

- **The Federal Emergency Management Agency**

1-800-621-FEMA (*www.fema.gov*)

- **Where to Go for Government Disaster Help**

One of the first places to go for information related to disaster management, response and recovery is: *http://www.disasterhelp.gov.*

- **Federal Citizen Information Center (FCIC)**

For questions about federal agencies, programs, benefits and services, you can call 1-800-FED-INFO (1-800-333-4636).

- **National Flood Insurance Program**

www.floodsmart.gov/floodsmart/pages/index.jsp
The NFIP is a cooperative effort between the federal government and private insurance companies.

- **Home Mortgage Insurance**

If your home was destroyed or significantly damaged by a presidentially declared natural disaster, you may be eligible for home mortgage insurance offered through the Department of Housing and Urban Development (HUD) working through approved lenders.

The main HUD website is *http://www.hud.gov*. The Disaster Voucher Program (DVP) can be accessed at *http://www.hud.gov/news/dvp.cfm*.

- **Small Business Disaster Relief Loans**

If you have a small business that was impacted by a presidentially declared natural disaster, you may qualify for a disaster relief loan through the Small Business Administration.

CONTACT INFORMATION FOR THE SBA is:

Small Business Administration
409 3rd Street, SW
Washington, DC 20416
(202) 205-6734 Office of Disaster Assitance
(800) 659-2955 Customer Service
www.sba.gov

- **Federal Assistance to Individual and Households Program (IHP)**

You may be eligible for FEMA grants for housing assistance and other disaster-related expenses such as personal property, transportation, medical, dental or funeral expenses. Go to website:
http://www.fema.gov/media/fact_sheets/individual-assistance.shtm

- **FEMA Temporary Housing Program**

http://www.fema.gov/assistance/process/assistance.shtm
is the website to go to if you are possibly eligible for this assistance.

MORTGAGE AND RENTAL ASSISTANCE PROGRAM

If you have received notice of eviction or foreclosure due to financial hardship resulting from a disaster, you may be eligible for assistance under this program.

- **Rental Assistance**

If your home has become unlivable due to a disaster, whether you are a homeowner or renter, you may apply for this rental assistance.

- **Minimal Repairs Program**

If your home has minor damages but is unlivable as a direct result of a disaster, you may be eligible for money through this program.

- **Disaster Unemployment Assistance**

If you lose your job as a result of a disaster and are not eligible for regular unemployment insurance compensation, you may be eligible for this asistance and receive weekly subsidy. If you think you may be eligible for this assistance,
go to: *www.workforcesecurity.doleta.gov/unemploy/disaster.asp*

- **Emergency Food Coupons**

You may be eligible for food coupons following a disaster based on your need. The U.S. Department of Agriculture and state authorities administer this program.

APPENDIX M

NATIONAL VOLUNTARY ORGANIZATIONS ACTIVE IN DISASTER

For more information about NVOAD, go to the following site: *www.nvoad.org.* For a list of members, go to: *http://www.nvoad.org/membersdb.php?members=National.*

MEMBER LIST

Adventist Community Services
America's Second Harvest
American Baptist Men
American Radio Relay League
American Red Cross
AMURT (Ananda Marga Universal Relief Team)
Catholic Charities USA
Center for International Disaster Information
Christian Disaster Response International
Christian Reformed World Relief Committee
Church of the Brethren—Emergency Response/Service Ministries
Church World Service
Convoy of Hope
Disaster Psychiatry Outreach
Episcopal Relief and Development
Friends Disaster Service, Inc.
The Humane Society of the United States
International Aid
International Critical Incident Stress Foundation
International Relief Friendship Foundation
Lutheran Disaster Response
Mennonite Disaster Service
Mercy Medical/Angel Flight America
National Emergency Response Teams (NERT)
National Organization for Victim Assistance
Nazarene Disaster Response
Northwest Medical Teams International

Points of Light Foundation & Volunteer Center National Network
Presbyterian Church (U.S.A.)
REACT International, Inc.
The Salvation Army
Society of St. Vincent de Paul
Southern Baptist Convention—North American Mission Board
United Jewish Communities
United Church of Christ—Wider Church Ministries
United Methodist Committee on Relief (UMCOR)
United Way of America
Volunteers of America
World Vision

Members of State/County/City VOADs Also Providing Services

Christian Appalachian Project
Christian Contractors Association (FLVOAD)
United Jewish Federation of New York

Friends of VOAD

Church of Jesus Christ of Latter Day Saints
Compassion Alliance
Hope Coalition America
Samaritan's Purse International Relief

RECOMMENDED READING AND WEB SITES

Publications giving hazard specific preparedness guidelines include:

Andrews, Harris J. and Bowers, J. Alexander. *The Pocket Disaster Survival Guide.* Accokeek, MD: Stoeger Publishing Company, 2006.

Are You Ready? An in-depth Guide to Citizen Preparedness, published by the Department of Homeland Security/FEMA. Call 1-800-BE-READY or visit the DHS web site *www.ready.gov.* This publication is free.

Beren, Norris L. *When Disaster Strikes Home!* Mt. Prospect, IL: Emergency Preparedness Educational Institute Publishing, 2004.

Deyo, Holly Drennan. Dare to Prepare! Pueblo West, CO: Deyo Enterprises, 2004-2007.

Edwards, Anton. *Preparedness No*w! An Emergency Survival Guide for Civilians and Their Families. Los Angeles, CA: Process Media, 2006.

Kolberg, Judith. *Organize for Disaster.* Decatur, GA: Squall Press, 2004.

Neuenschwander, Mark, M.D., and Neuenschwander, Betsy, M.D. *Crisis Evangelism, Preparing to be Salt and Light When the World Needs Us Most.* Ventura, CA: Regal Books/A Division of Gospel Light, 1999.

Suggested Emergency Preparedness Supplies Websites

www.nitro-pak.com: emergency preparedness supplies
www.beprepared.com: emergency preparedness supplies
www.areyouprepared.com: emergency preparedness center
www.emprep.com: emergency preparedness kits and supplies
www.solarsense.com: emergency power systems
www.sundancesolar.com: solar energy products
www.technonllc.com: emergency escape mask
www.aquamira.com: essentials for water purification products

Special Information Related to the H1N1 (Swine Flu) Pandemic

Projections of the number of people who will become ill from the H1N1 virus vary widely. A recent report indicates up to 50 percent of the U.S. population will become infected and up to 90,000 will die. The truth is that no one knows for sure.

There is concern that the H1N1 virus could mutate and become more virulent. It is also possible that the virus could become resistant to the Tamiflu (oseltamivir) and Relenza (zanamivir) that at the present time are usually effective against the swine flu. Should you develop flu-like symptoms, contact your health care provider immediately.

Vitamin D Deficiency and the Relationship to Influenza

Vitamin D plays a significant role in achieving healthy immune system. Studies have shown that individuals with higher vitamin D levels are less likely to contract influenza. That is one of the reasons many people get the flu in the winter and spring when exposure to sunlight is the lowest.

MAJOR ALERT!

In a recent study it was reported that 7 out of 10 U.S. children are Vitamin D-insufficient! African-Americans and Mexican-Americans, as well as pregnant women, also lack sufficient Vitamin D. Currently 400 IU/day of vitamin D is recommended for children and adolescents. Even more is recommended for pregnant women. Take vitamin D and get at least 20-30 minutes of sun daily, if possible!

Elderberry Extract

A recent study reported that Sambucol, a standardized extract of black elderberry has been found to fight avian flu virus (H5N1). Elderberry extracts have been used for years to help treat flu symptoms. According to this study, those taking elderberry supplements recovered in half the time.

H1N1 Vaccinations

I briefly address the issue of a vaccine for the H1N1 (swine flu) on page 54. I do not support compulsory vaccinations. Each person must make an informed decision for himself/herself and their families.

Dr. Williams and Dr. Duininck coordinating the
Indonesian and American disaster relief teams

Man going through the rubble of his home after tsunami devastation

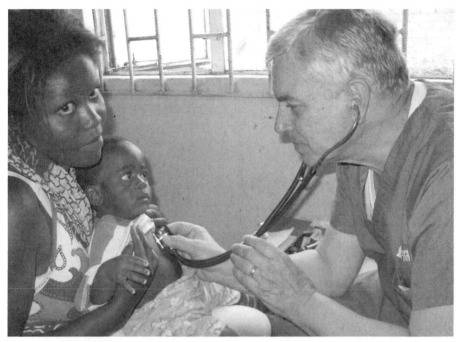

Dr. Williams examiming the baby of a grateful mother

Dr. Williams with Paul Wilbur and Dr. Saforo during Shalom Zambia outreach

Contact Information About Author

To contact the author to speak at your organization, conference, or church,
please write to:

Paul R. Williams, M.D.

International HealthCare Network

P.O. Box 1180

Pisgah Forest, NC 28768

or email:

ihndoc@yahoo.com

For more information visit:

www.whenallplansfail.com

THE MISSION

Prepare individuals, neighborhoods and churches to take responsibility for their own preparedness for emergencies and disasters.

Facilitate organizations to respond rapidly to major disasters with humanitarian aid, medical teams, and compassionate ministry.

Mobilize medical teams to bring hope and healing through the love of Jesus to hurting, impoverished people around the world.

Raise Up and Equip the next generation of compassionate ministry leaders.

Integrate the truths of divine healing with practical medicine to meet physical and spiritual needs of others.

Encourage healthcare professionals to use their skills in ministry.

Challenge leaders to greater collaboration for more effective ministry.

Paul Williams, M.D.
setting up a clinic in India

International HealthCare Network

When the tsunami struck in Indonesia, we were there!

Help us respond to disasters by supporting International HealthCare Network (501c3).
P O Box 1180, Pisgah Forest, NC 28768 E-mail: ihndoc@yahoo.com

Congratulations to
Dr. Paul Williams!

CORNERSTONE TELEVISION NETWORK
CONGRATULATES DR. PAUL WILLIAMS
ON THE THIRD PRINTING OF "WHEN ALL PLANS FAIL"

Through the *Hope Connection*, CTVN has been able to
reach around the world to bring hope to the "least of these"...
the broken, abandoned and abused children of the world.

- 700,000 meals were fed
- Thousands rescued from disease,
  malnutrition, war, and slavery

For these children, "all other plans have failed".
200 Million are abandoned right now. With your help,
we can make one more *Hope Connection* for a child in need.

THE HOPE CONNECTION
CORNERSTONE TELEVISION   1 SIGNAL HILL DR.   WALL, PA 15148-1499
412-824-3930   WWW.CTVN.ORG

Tsunamis... hurricanes... tornados... floods... man-made disasters...

Have you wanted to help, but just didn't know how?

Hope Force International prepares Christians—spiritually and pragmatically— to respond with compassion to those affected by disaster... and provides a pathway of service.

Come join our growing ranks of disaster responders... There's a place waiting for you!

HOPEFORCE INTERNATIONAL®

(615) 371-1271

info@hopeforce.org
www.hopeforce.org

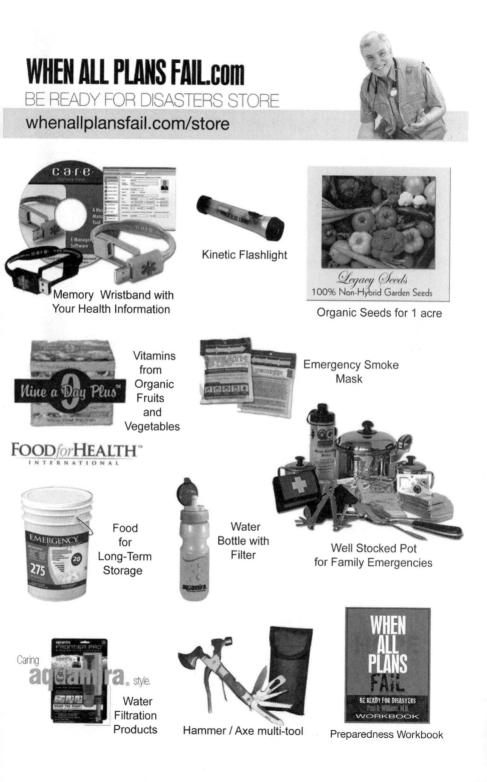

NETWORK FOR BETTER NUTRITION

OUR PURPOSE

To acquire nutritious food products directly from farms and other food producers, by donation and or purchase. To also develop and produce new products. All products acquired or produced are to be distributed at no cost to local food banks, kitchens that provide free meals to low income seniors, children, and the homeless. Food products will also be provided to disaster relief organizations. Also to provide Nutritional Education programs to public and private elementary and secondary schools, that encourage students to choose highly nutritious food products that were grown and or produced with the least impact on the environment.

GROWERS AND PRODUCERS:
Surplus food urgently needed NOW.
We will accept shipments or when possible come to your location to pickup.
All types of food products needed for our food programs serving seniors, children and disaster relief victims.

TOP 5 REASONS TO SUPPORT AND DONATE

-It's safe and legal - Good Samaritan laws protect donors.
-You may be able to reduce the cost of your garbage bill.
-Your business will help reduce hunger and waste.
-Your donations may be tax deductible.
-Your donation boosts employee morale and strengthens
  community relationships.

For information on how you can assist the Network for Better Nutrition:
Call our office at: (863)965-1800 or Email Director at
Director@networkforbetternutrition.org

A MESSAGE FROM AUTHOR PAUL R. WILLIAMS, M.D.
TO ALL WHO ARE WISELY PREPARING FOR DISASTERS

As a physician with more than twenty-five years of medical mission and disaster relief experience, my goal is to equip believers to proactively prepare individually and as a community of believers for natural and man-made disasters. Flooding, hurricanes, tornadoes and earthquakes are increasing in frequency. Also, the threat of terrorism on our soil is ever before us.

Unexpected disasters can add to the personal and societal stresses that we all experience in these changing times. Being prepared spiritually, mentally, and physically allows us to be part of the solution when disasters occur rather than being victimized. We also have a biblical mandate to be prepared.

Please consider hosting a seminar at your church or bringing several churches and community organizations together to sponsor a **When All Plans Fail Seminar**.

The **When All Plans Fail Seminar** is practical teaching on disaster preparedness from a Christian perspective. It is my belief that churches should be places of refuge at all times, especially in times of crisis.

Please let me help you get this important message out. Whether your church decides to host a seminar or not, I encourage you to use my book and workbook as a tool to lead small group studies in your home or in your church to prepare your family, friends and church members. **"The time to prepare is now!"**

To receive updates on disaster preparedness topics, events and **When All Plans Fail Seminars** contact me at: info@whenallplansfail.com.

For more information about our mission to prepare and equip believers and churches or to schedule a seminar or speaking engagement, contact me at: doctor@whenallplans.com or send correspondence to:
PO Box 1315, Pisgah Forest, NC 28768

Looking forward to hearing from you.

Paul R. Williams, M.D.

"A prudent man sees danger and takes refuge, but the simple keep going and suffer for it." Prov. 22:3

TWENTY-ONE DAYS:
Take One Action Item Each Day

BEGIN NOW! Take ONE action item each day. (See Chapter 11.)
By the end of twenty-one days, you will have completed the basic
requirements for disaster preparedness.

Day 1 Establish a schedule for disaster preparedness.

Day 2 Compile an emergency contact list.

Day 3 Make a list of early warning systems in your community.

Day 4 Identify your "horses," disasters common to your area.

Day 5 Write out your family communication plan in the event of disasters.

Day 6 Make copies of pictures of each family member; store where needed.

Day 7 Make neighborhood preparedness plans.

Day 8 Make lists of items to be included in your emergency kits.

Day 9 Make lists of long-term storage foods; schedule rotation.

Day 10 Make prescription meds list and set up rotation schedule.

Day 11 Make list of emergency supplies not stored in other kits.

Day 12 List first aid kit contents; insert first aid and CPR instructions.

Day 13 Make copies of appropriate important documents.

Day 14 Make copies of immunization records for each family member.

Day 15 Make copies of medical release forms for each child.

Day 16 Make evacuation plans with detailed maps and directions.

Day 17 Write instructions for care of special needs individuals.

Day 18 Make plans for escape routes for fires and post copies in bedrooms.

Day 19 Make plans for caring for animals and pets in emergencies.

Day 20 Establish a physical fitness program.

Day 21 Write out your nutritional goals.

YOU ARE WELL ON YOUR WAY TO BEING PREPARED!